Chas. R. Cooley.

PASTORAL
MINISTRY
to Families

Books by
JOHN CHARLES WYNN
Published by The Westminster Press

Pastoral Ministry to Families
How Christian Parents Face Family Problems

PASTORAL
MINISTRY
to Families

by
JOHN CHARLES WYNN

Philadelphia
THE WESTMINSTER PRESS

Library of Congress Catalog Card No.: 57–6553

PRINTED IN THE UNITED STATES OF AMERICA

TO
MY MOTHER

from whom I first knew
family love

CONTENTS

PREFACE

Some books are written in mountain hideaways that bear nostalgic references to places with quaint names like Snug Under the Hill or Lone Pine Rest. Such references look good in prefaces, but unfortunately this book can claim no such distinction. It has been written in bus stations, motel rooms, Pullman roomettes, and in the lower bunks of memorial cabins at several church camps. Most of it, however, was composed at our own home, in the third-floor study whose door sports a "Do Not Disturb" sign which nobody, but nobody, in our family takes seriously. Along with all the invasions for rubber bands, pencils, and toy repairs (as well as coffee deliveries), I've frequently and warmly recalled that when God set us in the midst of families he certainly did not intend it to be a solitary experience. There is something vaguely ironical about shutting yourself away from your family in order to write a book about the family anyway; and I'm grateful for the interruptions, and their company. Without them my knowledge of this subject would be scant indeed.

Gathered into the pages that follow are a representative selection of the major topics discussed over several years in a score of Pastors' Seminars in Family Counseling. Held in churches across the country, and on the campuses of such schools as Coe College, Huron College, and Iowa State University, these seminars have brought clergymen together to work through tough problems in family counseling. In a real, though sometimes perverse, way this book is a compilation of the ideas and memories from those days: real, because all those pastors helped to write these chapters by the way they contributed experiences and ideas in mutual education; perverse, because the interpretation hereinafter written occasionally represents an opinion that many of the pastors might reject. Certainly they cannot be held responsible for my own prejudices concerning wedding fees, ministers' families, the preaching of sermons, or " booby traps in counseling."

In larger measure, gratitude must be expressed to those leaders who participated in these seminars and imparted to them such inspiration and authority: Hugo A. Bourdeau, John Copp, William Crane, Clifford E. Davis, Roy E. Dickerson, Roy W. Fairchild, David M. Fulcomer, Richard N. Hey, James R. Hine, Paul B. Maves, Gelolo McHugh, Wayne E. Oates, F. Philip Rice, Donald F. Schroeder, David B. Treat, and Leland Foster Wood. With Tennyson's Ulysses, " I am a part of all that I have met "; and honesty compels me to acknowledge that these men and their insights are written across many of the pages in this book.

In the end, however, neither they nor the Board of Christian Education of the Presbyterian Church in the U.S.A., for which I work, can be held responsible for the content of this book. For it is not meant solely as a transcript of the Pastors' Seminars in Family Counseling, nor as an official interpretation of my Church's philosophy of Christian family education. The few case histories included in these chapters are elaborately disguised, even fictionalized. If they appear to describe some person or family in particular, it can only be because they are so typical.

In writing about the family, one is astounded by the magnitude of the theme and by the plethora of literature already published on the subject. Sociologists, psychologists, and religionists by the hundreds have set pen to paper to cover this theme; but there has been no one-volume work that pulls together the many facets of family ministry for the pastor. For all this talk of grace in family life, we do need handles to take hold of the task and to labor on specific problems; and this work is an attempt to supply such handles. The rapidly changing conditions in today's world have profoundly affected our families. New discoveries into the complex nature of human relationships have come from depth psychology and a broader grasp of sociology. New insights into

Biblical theology have shown that family relationships comprise a much more profound and basic concept for understanding the Christian message than we had previously dreamed.

To the many authors, colleagues, critics, and friends (these are overlapping categories) who have opened my eyes to such material, I am deeply grateful. The manuscript was read by Robert J. Cadigan, Roy W. Fairchild, John R. Fry, and George L. Hunt; from this quartet came many valuable suggestions. Particularly do I want to thank Elizabeth D. Benner, whose help as a typist and copy reader was outstanding. To Miss Selma M. Schad, who also assisted in manuscript preparation, and to Miss Merran Henry without whose services as a reference librarian not only I but many others would be directionless, I am deeply thankful. Last, though never least, my patient wife, Rachel, read and corrected many sections between her chores of motherhood on behalf of our three children, Mark, Maryan, Martha. God bless them!

J. C. WYNN

1

THE CHURCH
AS THE FAMILY OF GOD

HILDA: *First of all, I want to go round*
and look at all the things that
you have built. . . . Many church towers
among the rest? Immensely high ones?
SOLNESS: *No, I build no more church towers now.*
Nor churches either.
HILDA: *What do you build then?*
SOLNESS: *Homes for human beings.*
HILDA: (reflectively): *Couldn't you build a*
little — a little bit of a church
tower over these homes as well?

From *The Master Builder,* by Henrik Ibsen.

Theology, contrary to popular notion, is born less often in the quiet study of contemplative divines than in the heat and rigor of life's arenas. The great body of Christian theology has been evolved from problems that cried for solution, from emergencies that necessitated succor. Far from despising this process, church-men have learned that some of our most relevant doctrines and our most valued insights have emerged just this way. God re-veals himself not only through the blessed visions perceived in some saint's mystical moments but also in the hurly-burly of hu-man relations. God speaks through history; and some of the most difficult historical situations have given rise to our greatest doc-trines when Christians prayerfully wrestled with the issues of their time.

In just this manner, the concept of " the Church as a family "

13

first emerged. Paul the apostle, who thought of himself as missioner and might have been astonished to hear himself called (as now he is) an abstract theologian, coined the term " *household* of God." This phrase, which can be justifiably translated also as " *family* of God," is applied to certain churches of Galatia. There some of the Christian community was rent by intense, even vicious, rivalry between Judaizers and Gentiles. In his attempt to bind these warring factions together the apostle showed them that they all belong to one family in the Church, the family of God. To these people, such words rang less quaintly than they do upon our modern ear. In their experience, there were no church buildings. The fellowship met for worship in the homes of the people. Paul occasionally referred to a familiar circumstance, " the church in your house," as he wrote letters to his friends. The concept of the Church as a family, indeed of the family itself as a small church, was not the fantasy of dreamy doctrinarians. It grew out of a common situation, and the idea took hold. Now, centuries later, this figure of speech seems more appropriate than ever before. Although we know other metaphors for the Church, e.g., " the bride of Christ " or " the body of Christ," one of the most suggestive of all is " the Church as a family."

Strikingly parallel to the human family in a number of ways, the Church through the centuries has been both a family of believers and a family of families.

The Church, for instance, is known in the New Testament as the ecclesia, " those who are called out." Central to the meaning of this word is the idea that in this calling we did not choose, but we were chosen. We were brought together in a communal group not of our making, and without our consent. The Church, and the family as well, is composed of members who did not organize it. It was established before our time, and we were summoned to it by a power greater than ourselves. In a profound sense, neither can we escape so firm a hold upon us. We may quit a family relationship, but we cannot ever be rid of family connections. We may try to run away, but the family's claim is ever upon us. This relationship we did not construct; and we cannot destroy it. Neither the Church nor the family was formed by us. Both are of God.

The Church and the family are similar in another respect: each accepts people for themselves rather than for what they have achieved. This is idealistic talk, to be sure. Yet when the Church is truly the Church, as when the family is behaving according to its own peculiar genius, both are remarkable for their acceptance. They provide a loving acceptance in spite of the unworthy performance their members sometimes exhibit and in each case there is a profound sense of brotherhood. Reuel L. Howe, in his inspired book *Man's Need and God's Action,* tells, for instance, of a church board that kept in contact with one of their members after he had been convicted and imprisoned for a crime. It had not been easy to accept either him or his guilt. But they had prayed through this problem to see their way as a fellowship. When he was released from prison, they with their pastor awaited him at the gate and received him again. The next few years of readjustment were difficult for him, yet through that time he knew that he had the understanding (in the sense of their " standing under ") from his brothers in Christ. This again is a family characteristic, for both home and Church are agents of God's loving, yet just, acceptance.

Thirdly, the Church is also a family that feeds its own. As in the home, we have here a table spread for our nourishment, the Table of the Lord. We feed upon his Word; we know him through our senses — " O taste and see that the Lord is good." Indeed our most profound sacrament in Christendom is the Holy Supper, wherein we bring the fellowship together for thanksgiving and a sacred meal. There is reason to believe that the earliest Communion observance was part of a love feast celebrated in prayer and thanksgiving at the homes of the Christians. This practice is pregnant with meaning for us today. As John Oliver Nelson says, " Even the Holy Supper on Sundays, in a special building set apart, is only a poignant and reassuring reminder that there is a Host who is present at our every daily meal " (*Kirkridge Contour,* June, 1956). The Early Church was undoubtedly found in the sharing of bread inside the homes of the people of the Way, truly *ecclesia domestica*. By this act they found themselves bound together in a veritable household of faith. Now psychologists agree (an unusual concurrence) that the human personality first learns to love through reception of food. The infant, unlearned in the ways of affection, early receives unearned and unrequested love when he feeds at his mother's breast. So too the Christian begins to comprehend something of the family of God as he receives God's undeserved outgoing, forgiving love. This is nowhere better dramatized than in that Eucharistic rite that is Holy Communion.

Fourthly, the Church resembles a family as it becomes a fellowship of mutual assistance. Admittedly, here again we must speak in terms of the normative (that which should be) rather than strictly in terms of the descriptive (that which we usually find). But in its best expression, the Church as a family is open to unlimited liability for its members. The Church of the Savior in Washington, D.C., has been a thrilling example of a sacrificial Christian society. Within their community no member feels alone. He is undergirded in his need by a group who will go the whole way, giving cloak as well as coat to him as he needs. Their procedure includes an arrangement to aid one another in the building of houses, assistance in mortgages, subsidy in time of illness and hospitalization, and ceaseless spiritual support in the problems of daily living. Here in this example of the hospitality of the saints is a picture of the family of God going about its everyday business of mutual help, truly a priesthood of all believers. Drawing together like a family, they close their ranks and assist one another where assistance is needed.

The Christian Church also comprises a family fellowship for some who have no blood family ties. If God in his providence has set the solitary in families, in his wisdom he has also provided a family in the Church for those who have no blood ties left, or whose own household is unfriendly to the Church. The Church gathers up the lonely, the aged, the bereft and brings to them comfort and consolation. It is passing strange that in our new zeal for family participation in the churches, some pastors have neglected the unmarried, the widowed, the lonely, and the unaccepted. We can so emphasize "the family program" of the parish that those who have no mate or children feel unwanted and frozen out. What denial of the family principle this is! Let the Church enfold its whole family in loving acceptance lest lonely members fail to comprehend the loving will of God because of our failure to consider the needs of such individuals.

The House Church

Canon Ernest Southcott, of Leeds, has revived "the Church in your house" concept in so radical a way that this ancient standard appears entirely new and succeeds in the way that only new things can. In a brief fourteen-page broadsheet, as the English call it, he describes this venture as a revival of apostolic Christianity. The course of early Christianity was spread from house to house, as he says, just in the manner of plagues. And now, faith, like a plague, is sweeping through the parish of Leeds. They now hold confirmation classes in their neighborhood homes, celebrate Holy Communion on the kitchen tables of numerous apartments, and try in every way to return the Church to the people. Some might fear that this delivery service would keep the people away from the sanctuary henceforth and forever. Not so, writes Canon Southcott; the people come back to the Church with a new sense of communion and of meeting (*The House Church,* by Ernest W. Southcott).

Simultaneously in the country to the north, the Iona community has penetrated the Church of Scotland with a new ideal of evangelism carried to whole family groups. As described in that community's magazine, *The Coracle,* deeply significant neighborhood meetings of families have been a part of the "Tell Scotland" campaign of evangelism. This idea has been startling to many whose concept of the Church is confined to a building. "It's an effort of the imagination for us to realize that the Early Church had no buildings but met only in the houses of its members. The invitation of our evangelism is 'to come to church' and in the minds alike of church people and those outside, that means to come to a building." (*The Coracle,* March, 1956.) The Iona community for years has worked on the principle that the true Church has to be found where its people are — in their homes and in their work. Not a new idea at all, this reiterates a principle of the Early Church and re-emphasizes a title the Protestant Reformers gave to the family: *ecclesia in ecclesiola*, " a little church within the Church."

Given the context of their Church doctrine, perhaps the most revolutionary concept of a " Church in your house " has occurred in a Roman Catholic parish in Paris. The unusual, thrilling story of such an experiment is to be found in Abbé G. Michonneau's *Revolution in a City Parish*. Fr. Michonneau and his staff of curates have evidently upset ecclesiastical tradition sufficiently for the cardinal to write a qualifying preface to the book, cautioning the reader to gain approval from superiors before launching so novel a plan. What the Parisian priests had done in their parish is parallel to what the English and Scots had done in theirs — they made a direct apostolate to the homes of the people. They had noted that parishioners brought their infants to the font for Baptism in the spirit that they took the same children to the physician for vaccination. In a successful attempt to put an end to this sacrilege, Fr. Michonneau and his colleagues turned the parish upside down through religious education of families — right in their own homes. He testifies: " We went into every home and talked religion frankly and proudly and lovingly — and usually we were more than welcome. Some came back to Christ on the spot " (p. 105).

What was done in these three parishes is cited here simply because they are in scattered points, and they have been formulated into written reports. That the same or even more effective work has been done in American parishes is not denied. What is more encouraging is that such innovations are on the increase; pastors and official boards are launching into programs that are encouragingly relevant to today's problems. The East Harlem Protestant Parish, the Church of the Savior in Washington (cited above), and many other churches have begun to make inroads into establishing the kind of house church that Paul would recognize as natural.

As this point of view grows in influence, a new vitality can confidently be expected in the Christian community. As we return to the Pauline " Church in your home " concept, we actually enter a new era that could drastically shake both home and Church as we know them now.

The Church Misunderstands the Family

With all the new interest in family life, our Church leadership still remains amazingly out of touch with family realities. Although we try hard, and we think we understand our families from experience, study, and observation, we are capable of widely missing the mark.

Item: One large denomination took a survey of its clergymen, asking them to cite the three most common areas of discord among married couples in their parishes. Promptly the clergy replied: the big three are drinking, sex difficulties, and religious disagreements. Then the survey was turned to the married couples themselves; and the selfsame question was asked. Their own reply about themselves was startlingly different: the big three disagreements concern money, in-laws, and child training!

Item: Sociologists turn up one persistent finding about church families with disturbing frequency. There appears only a modest correlation between Church pronouncements about how families ought to live and how they actually live. Rigorous regulations concerning divorce and remarriage are easily skirted by canny parishioners who get their divorces and then go elsewhere for their succeeding nuptials. Dire warnings about interfaith marriage apparently frighten but few of those who are adding to an increasing trend of interfaith matrimony. The counseling pastor too knows how little effect the Churches' teachings about sex ethics have influenced some of the laity.

Item: While howling about the divisiveness of community life, and the way that multifarious demands intrude upon the family, the Church turns around and repeats this condemned pattern. Our graded church school classes will likely split a family of five, five ways from Sunday. We separate each family at the church door according to gender and generation. Instead of being in the vanguard of those who weld the family together, the Churches too often join in the trend that disintegrates family solidarity. Few parishes could stand an impartial inquiry into what their organizations and activities are doing to family life through incessant requests for leadership and demands for support to strengthen institutional programs. It would be hard to estimate how many such programs could die without harm to the parish; but it seems clear that many of them are kept alive only by dint of unnecessary sacrifice from the unwary membership. Many of these long-suffering families never stop to ask whether it is mere blind tradition or someone's ego needs that perpetuate the bowling league, the rummage sales, and the Tuesday Night Discussion Society.

Item: Although there is a resurgence in religious interest as well as a new enthusiasm for familism, these benefits have not cut so deeply as we might wish. One testimonial, which just may be typical of thousands, is found in *The Family,* by Ernest W. Burgess and Harvey J. Locke (p. 510). Says a young mother quoted by the authors: "Our family is much more liberal. We hold a proper reverence for God, but realize, through our more advanced knowledge, that many unusual events, supernatural to our grandparents, are not directly attributable to Him. This understanding of the world and nature removes many of the fears that oppressed our grandparents. Our philosophy of living in the family group is not restriction and self-denial but rather pleasure and self-expression. We never have prayer before meals because we are always in too big a hurry. No one is home in the evenings for family prayers. There are too many places to go on Sundays, or we were out too late Saturday evening; so consequently we do not always go to church."

Item: Laymen take clergymen and their family ministry somewhat less seriously than the clergy do themselves. Britain's irreverent *New Statesman and Nation* once defined "Clerastianism" as: "That heresy which accepts the supremacy of the clergy in family affairs. Members of the sect submit their infants to ceremonial head-wetting while placing the tongue in a ritual position in the cheek, precede their nuptial rites by ancient formulae to which they make mental reservations, and bury their ancestors only after a ceremony which they believe will ensure respectability if not immortality."

Where the Church Is Inadequate for Its Families

Modernization ever lags behind need. The churches of America are fully aware that a new day has dawned in family education. Yet in many areas we insist on an impossible program, attempting to accommodate a nineteenth century pattern to an atomic era. For new church plants we lay out acres of parking space so that families may drive from appreciable distances and park their station wagons; but what they discover inside the church may be a continuation of an outdated schedule when parishioners came to church in surreys. Although we are aware of the family ideal of togetherness in contemporary America, many of our churches still make it difficult for the entire family to attend at the same time, compelling them instead to shuttle back and forth in shifts to attend meetings that duplicate and conflict with one another. The church that sets up conflicting meetings, that omits nursery care from its plans and thus penalizes younger families, or that offers a worship service aimed only at the understanding of adults and expects the family auto to track back and forth like a trolley car is less inviting families than it is victimizing them.

Church edifices are erected to house the ever-growing crowds of larger families; the increasing population so strains the facilities that by the time they are dedicated it is discovered that they have met only yesterday's needs. No church building can confine all of our Christian education and life. Until church planners and architects face the practical validity of the doctrine of the household of faith, they will continue to wrestle with building funds, attempting the impossible — to perform an educational task that can better be accomplished at home. The sad fact is that many of our churches are out of touch with the real needs of the families on their rolls. Protestantism, still geared to a nineteenth century rural pattern of organization in many of its city and suburban churches, falls far short of meeting present needs. This way lies failure.

Uncovering some of the inadequacies of the churches' work with parish families, a project of the National Council of Churches under the direction of Richard E. Lentz has listed these:

1. Churches need to develop a hospitality program to " shepherd " new families into the fellowship.

2. Official boards need to take cognizance of the unserved types of families, e.g., all-adult households, the broken homes (perhaps one in seven church families is broken by death or divorce), and the divided families whose religious loyalties stretch over two or more parishes.

3. Parishes still overlook the welfare of older families in their midst, those who need help regarding retirement, housing arrangements, and an antidote for loneliness.

4. Churches are not geared to aiding the family with mental illness or a physical sickness at home.

5. Our churches are not often aware of the types of family ministry that they should be performing to the aged, to those in trouble, and to those who need guidance.

6. Ministers need to improve their premarital counseling work beyond a one-session discussion of wedding arrangements.

7. Churches frequently overlook the community agencies that could work with them as a team to aid families with difficulties.

8. Most churches do not see their opportunities in public service projects such as establishing co-operative nursery schools, maternal health groups, counseling clinics, and scores of other services.

When the Church Is Indifferent to Families

Jean Schick Grossman, parent educator and author, tells of the man who attended church when the preacher was feelingly expounding the tragic circumstances of one family's sorrow. Alone among all the people in the congregation this man remained dry-eyed and unmoved at the recital of their plight. When he walked out of the church, someone asked him why he hadn't been touched by the story. He replied, " I don't belong to this parish."

Verily there is a parochial attitude on the part of many church members to the needs of families in their neighborhood. One pastor reports that he has been unsuccessful in getting his people to call on strangers and migrant families in the very same block as the church. The excuse of his calling committees has usually been, " Why, they'll probably be here only about six months." This kind of unfeeling outlook is not surprising to anyone intimately familiar with the seamier side of contemporary church life. Reuben Hill's *Families Under Stress* reports that when the veterans of World War II returned home they did not find the churches especially compassionate at this crucial time, nor their families especially responsive to the churches. One incident cited in the book concerns a family in which four children became sick at one time. No physician would call on them until the relief office would give approval, because they lacked a good credit rating. What is worse, however, was that " during this period of stress no church organization came to their aid " (p. 287).

The vast misery that families experience at times of physical and emotional illness, of alcoholism, of financial reverses, dissension, and adversity can be seen in the constituency of every church. It is a rare church, however, that is organized to do more than send an already overworked pastor to call on the household. The onetime compassion of the early Christians will not be recovered until the Church as a whole becomes responsive to such needs, and until it sees in these adversities family-wide implications that need a healing touch of a committed fellowship.

In this connection, it might be very wise for official boards in parish churches to declare a moratorium on the organizing of any new groups. We Americans are sometimes guilty of the accusation hurled at us by an English cleric: " You are always building expensive staircases that no one wants to go up." The serious fact is that our very organizations tend to break up the family unity that we praise. Father goes to men's class, mother to the ladies' guild, sister to the junior choir, brother to the intermediates. The church can be a divisive organization, tearing apart the family by unthinking enthusiasm for special groups. On the other hand, those churches are to be commended that consider men's work, for instance, to be what a man does in his total church life rather than what he does in a men's meeting which requires him periodically to come out of his home and away from his family. Some churches even recognize that Sunday evening is an ideal time for family life, and therefore schedule no Sunday night youth meetings, choosing rather to do their work with youth at a time when it does not jeopardize family solidarity.

Further to emphasize its responsibility for the Christian family, the Church might return to a method of counting membership that was once rather widely used. It is still continued in the churches of Northern Ireland. There a parish is considered to be a community of families, and its enrollment is numbered not by individuals but by family units. The local church does not have a membership of 852 individuals; it is composed of 390 families. Families are defined in terms of household relationships — parents and children living together or a grown son with his father, or a husband and wife, or a single person living alone. Plainly this method views the Church as made up of people in relationship to each other, rather than as disconnected individuals taking part in some program. For the basic unit of any parish is not its organizations, but the families.

The Atypical Family

Concentrating on the primacy of the family in Christian education does, however, create the danger of the Church neglecting the problems of people outside " average family " life. The Church must shun those stereotypes of thinking that leave no place for the unmarried adult and seem to imply that the only abundant fulfillment of life is in marriage, and with children. Churches might copy the Census Bureau's definition of the family as " two or more people related by blood or adoption living under the same roof." To those whose lives do not include the boodle of apron, fireplace, tricycles, and slippers, the churches also have a duty.

There are atypical families who could be forgotten in an enthusiastic Christian family life program, for this emphasis concentrates upon the usual home configuration of father, mother, and children, and rightly so. Nonetheless a church education program exclusively organized around such people will certainly increase the loneliness and isolation of those who already feel the want for close family ties: the unmarried, the widowed, the divorced, or in some instances unwed mothers. Those who have married outside their faith and still keep contact with their own church might be all but neglected by a program that is exclusively limited to the whole family, because the remainder of their family may be enrolled in quite another tradition. Families who live out of reach, those who are overseas for a year, those who reside in distant rural areas, those whose health or employment prevent participation in the regular program: for such atypical families another type of ministry will be needed.

Fortunately, many adult programs are aimed at serving this sizable segment of our parish memberships: young adult groups for single people, men's clubs that provide for fellowship of married and single men, businesswomen's guilds, older adults' fellowships (where " single " status means also the widowed). Home departments serve many of the shut-ins and the shift workers. Such activities are to be found in the churches of any denomination. But organized programs are not enough. More and more, our preaching and teaching program, our training in worship, and our patterns of thinking need to consider all of our constituency as the church family.

Organizing Our Pastoral Work

Vocabulary usages among the civil service employees of Washington are rich and unusual. Among the suggestive terms that have crept into their vocabulary in recent years is one that expresses the unimportant but impressive-looking work of administrators. They call this " administrivia." The term can be as easily applied to the work of many ministers.

If pastors were paid either by the hour or by piecework, most of them would command a higher income than they now receive. Pastors lead busy lives. From early morning until late at night, and even when an emergency arises in the middle of the night also, the hard-working pastor is at his job. His day includes devotions, study, and calling, plus the thousand and one little things that consume hours: mimeographing and mailing, bake sales and basketball leagues, shopping for light bulbs, and errands for the scouts. Most of these latter items come under the new hybrid word " administrivia."

Administrivia can so fill his days that the average clergyman must fight somehow to fulfill his vocation. Because he has so many things to do, he stands constantly in danger of losing sight of his main purpose. To add then another obligation to the ministry seems as heartless as it is futile. The only justification for any new emphasis in this already full job would be that it might offer a lift instead of a load.

Organizing the parish ministry around the family provides just that sort of lift. Preaching and pastoral work, committee assignments and administrative detail, counseling, leadership training, Christian education, worship, and recreation all take on new meaning and integration when seen in the context of the family. The parson who is chained to the daily treadmill of fatiguing activity and administrivia has two steps to take: (1) the organizing of his daily work around the integrating principle of ministering to Christian families; and then (2) the training of parents and leaders of the parish to work at their God-given task. For some this is a radical reorientation; but in that direction lies a rewarding pastorate.

It is when the clergyman commits himself to his central task that he appreciates the wisdom of organizing the great part of his work around a ministry to families. Any pastor in his right mind looks askance at new jobs and duties for his already too heavy schedule. If the pastoral care of families were just another load to carry in that schedule, it would have to be met with severe doubts.

No pastor alone, however, could hope to minister adequately to the needs of his parish families. In so huge an assignment he needs help. Unless he recruits and trains others who can aid in carrying on this family ministry, his pastoral work cannot succeed. Among the homes on the church roll are persons who can share in this task. In the main this is a job for adult education. The best educators in our churches are parents; and the finest schools for Christian living are the homes of our people. An investment of time and effort in training them will pay off handsome dividends in the future. Robert Maynard Hutchins has recently advocated that we empty our public schools of children and replace them in the classrooms with adults because we are too near the zero hour of civilization to continue traditional forms of education.

Clarifying Our Theology

To be effective, however, our family life ministry greatly needs a thorough grounding in Biblical theology. For a long time we have left untouched vast areas of Biblical doctrine concerning the family. Historically, God has spoken to man through man; the message of revelation has been given to people, some of them being quite ordinary folk, who then pass it on to still others. It is simple enough to see what this means in terms of the home where the incoming generation is indoctrinated in nearly all things by the parents. Theirs is the precious responsibility of communicating their faith to little children. The fact that this is done not only by means of words but in the language of relationships, through emotional overtones, among habitual actions, and in the manner that our needs are provided remains a truism still missed by many families.

Frightening as these implications are at first to the parents, their later reaction is one of comfort. When parents come to see that their unconscious mannerisms are soaked up by imitative offspring, it becomes plain to them that by doing their best in personal life they also do the best job of rearing the young. Parents plainly could use more encouragement than they have been getting from the Church.

If the Church were not already supplied with so great an asset in its parents, we would be compelled to go to considerable expense to provide a suitable substitute. These educators, teachers by nature, at first glance do not appear to be so proficient. They are of all kinds and have all sorts of abilities. Somehow in God's unaccountable reasoning, the world's most exacting task of bringing the next generation into maturity is assigned to these rank amateurs we know as fathers and mothers. Mere parents, none of them very expert, and even the best of them woefully imperfect, have clearly been elected to the stewardship of parent-hood, a job they simply dare not muff.

Inexcusably tardy in applying the insights of Biblical theology to family education, the Church has often operated its parent program as an inadequate imitation of the public school's parent-teacher association. As if this pattern fitted church life, the ecclesiastics have piled one obligation on top of another and vaguely inferred that their fulfillment would produce a Christian family. Such heresy! That the parlaying of good works such as daily worship, grace at table, bedtime prayers, and general good will could make a family Christian is tantamount to insisting that an individual can be saved by his own merit. We clergymen frequently refer to the doctrine of justification by faith for individuals. *The family, just as the individual, is justified by faith.* It is only through the grace of God that a family comes to be Christian; and no system of self-help techniques will serve instead. But when God has been permitted to work his will in a home, the fruits of the Spirit can be seen in the relationships of those people and in the works that they do. When the import of this truth first makes impact upon people, a confusion always results. It was so in the time of Paul, of Augustine, and climactically of Martin Luther. Yet justification by faith remains a wonderfully reassuring doctrine in family life as well as in personal life. It can be translated, as John Calvin once showed, in terms of acceptance (*Institutes of the Christian Religion,* III. ii. ii).

Imperfect though families are, they have this consolation — that the very same God whose loving care for children is recognized in Baptism is also the Father and the God of parents. Before him, indeed, we are all children. In his wisdom and goodness he has been able to use even our imperfections for his purpose. Errors we will make; but none of them are beyond redemption. Contrary to some opinions, the opportunities for the

training of children are not squandered by age five, or any other
arbitrary year; nor do parental mistakes ruin a youngster's entire
future. If sons and daughters have learned to look to parents for
support and for understanding, if, regardless of the tensions that
sometimes interfere with family life, their general impression of
home is that it is a place of love, we can thank God and take
courage. We can have faith in their future.

It is when our children receive this unselfish acceptance that
they experience the love through which God can make himself
known. The unstinting, undeserved, unrequested love an infant
receives from his mother prepares him to know what God's love
actually is. Love always takes the initiative: " We love, because
he first loved us."

As a matter of fact, the emotional life of the family has a de-
termining influence on the kind of faith the children will have. A
trusting faith is born in a family feeling where togetherness and
affection are part of the very air they breathe. The child who is
wanted, who is really loved, who is forgiven when rebellious and
helped when he fails, has the start toward strong mental health.
But what is more, he already has the groundwork for a firm
Christian faith.

Psychologists have a word for the tendency of parents to blame
both themselves and their children for inadequacies they themselves feel. They call this " projection," and it accounts for a host
of miserable households. In his provocative book *Man's Need
and God's Action,* Reuel L. Howe tells of a parent study group
that had come face to face with the awful truth that their children need more love than they were ever able to give them. Con-
fessing their weakness in this dilemma, they echoed Paul's, " O
wretched man that I am, who shall deliver me from this body of
death? " Then they adjourned and went their separate ways until the group met again the following week when — But let Professor Howe tell it in his own words:

". . . one of them said, ' You know, we got along better this week
than ever before.' To which another couple replied: ' You did? Isn't
that strange; so did we!' One by one they gave their witness that
the past week had been happier. This was surprising because each

had expected the opposite result. Intrigued, they began to inquire
about the cause of the unexpected result. The one reason for the im-
provement in their relations was, they discovered, the fact that for
the first time in their lives they had become aware of and had accepted some of the meaning of the truth that they were sinful, separated, finite beings and were unable, therefore, to love perfectly and
completely. They had not only been perfectionists, they had been god-
less perfectionists. They had assumed that they should and could do
all that was needed, and their inability to do so aroused in them an
anxiety that in the end produced in their families tension rather than
relaxation, irritability rather than peace, resentment rather than love "
(p. 91).

This experience of accepting our own imperfections and the
all-too-human features of our children is a pathway to forgiveness and it ought frequently to be featured in our preaching.
Without such an insight we are equally unable to forgive, or to
receive forgiveness. Forgiveness is learned at home if it is learned
at all; and there it must be a daily practice in the spirit of love
and understanding. Occasionally the pastor receives a confession
from some adult parishioner who testifies that he cannot feel that
God has forgiven him for his sins. And if the pastor then gently
inquires about the home life of that person, he may discover that
as a child *he never knew forgiveness at home.* His may have
been the mother who repeatedly used that damnable phrase, " If
you do that, Mother won't love you . . ." or, " I don't want such
a boy in my house . . ." et cetera, *ad nauseam.*

Jesus himself taught forgiveness in family terms, that God is
analogous to a father who day after day looks down a lonesome
road for his headstrong son until one great day that lad returns,
disheveled, broke, and ashamed. Then he welcomes him home,
reinstates him with new clothing, and celebrates the return of
his prodigal. In teaching about love, Jesus resorted again to
family life, reminding how a parent rejoices to give good things
to his children even as God the Father gives to his. Even the
spirit of the cross was interpreted in the language of parent-child
relationships, in necessitating the severing of the dearest bonds
earthly life knows for the sake of such sacrifice: " No one who

loves father or mother more than he loves me is worthy of me, and no one who loves son or daughter more than he loves me is worthy of me, and no one who will not take up his cross and follow me is worthy of me " (Matt. 10:37, 38). Over and again, the Master utilized the imagery of home life to interpret the Kingdom of God, telling of housewives at work, of children at play, of loyalty to parents. In that setting, these explanations were not lost upon hearers who had the Hebrew heritage of deep concern for family and clan. These were the people of the Deliverance, in whose homes the Passover was celebrated with children rehearsing God's goodness to his chosen people. " Why is this night different from all other nights? " the youngest would pipe. These were the families who reviewed the mighty Shema — " Hear, O Israel: the Lord our God is one Lord: and thou shalt love the Lord thy God with all thine heart, and with all thy soul, and with all thy might " (Deut. 6:4, 5). This word they recalled in conversation, in walks, in the morning and in the evening, in the costume they wore, and in the *décor* of their homes. Moreover, in that totalitarian state where lived the earliest Christians, most men had no political freedom or opportunity to be themselves in public affairs. But when they reached home, they were in a sanctuary, temporarily sheltered from the demands of a police state. There a man could be himself. When the Master spoke of family life, he struck chords of agreement and of hope.

Still, it would be far less than accurate to leave the impression that Jesus simply took advantage of a handy vocabulary of family life in order to clarify difficult doctrines about his Kingdom of Heaven. The family in his teaching, indeed in the plan of creation, is integral to the will of God. John Calvin enlarging on this in fact suggests that God ordained the family to protect his creation. Not until we begin to see something of God's family plan do we ever realize our deep roots of brotherhood, our hope for salvation (actually returning home to him), or our task in procreation, of creating *for* him. (See Chapter 6, " Christian Marriage and Marriage Counseling.")

Popular psychology features in our Sunday supplements deal overmuch in the dogma of " adjustment." This kind of emphasis

never reaches the heart of the matter, *viz.,* where our adjustment ultimately must be made. Our hearts are restless until they
find rest in God, as Augustine so long ago insisted. Those parents
whose Christian maturity has enabled them to find their way to
God in Christ can possess a self-acceptance and a depth of understanding that is valued above mere techniques of child management, or even those newly popular skills of group relations.

The anxieties of today's families are legion. If it were not so,
there would be fewer articles in our popular magazines and
newspapers (and fewer books for church educators) written
about family relationships. With this plethora of literature, it
must still be acknowledged that no amount of study in child
training will make up for lack of emotional instability in a
parent. No techniques mastered by a mother will replace the
spontaneous good relationships in a loving home. No grasp of
sociology will enable an insecure father to deal with the loneliness
and fears of his child when other children reject him. The
churches have to stop scolding parents for their inability to maintain some denominational par on the family course. This way
they have but added to the already burdensome guilt of parents,
and discouraged them still more. Families in the United States
are so infected with status anxieties (and perhaps that middle-
class group known as Protestants are worst of all), that their children become objects to manipulate for ambitious expectations and
higher ends. The amount of frustration and concern thus en-
gendered is incalculable. Hazards of parenthood are difficult
enough without added obstacles from the very fellowship that
could be of most help. It is the churches' task to encourage families, to lead them through worship to God their strength, to help
them with information and reassurance so that they might discover their own resources for the guidance of their children.
Thus Christian family life enters into its fullness. A family becomes a Christian family by the grace of God. Him they come
to know through their relationships and in their common worship. To that topic we must turn next.

2

THE FAMILY
IN COMMON WORSHIP

*Is your home a place of rest and
refreshment where God becomes more
real to those who enter it?*
— Query from the Friends' *Book of Discipline*.

A story that will not be quashed insists that when Dr. Henry
Sloan Coffin was pastor of New York City's Madison Avenue
Presbyterian Church, a well-dressed dowager gently chided him
for the mixed class of people who had begun to attend services
in response to his cordial welcome. Turning her nose toward the
gallery where a group of poor and some unwashed children had
been sitting, she sniffed: "Don't you detect a peculiar smell in
our church this morning?"

"That," Dr. Coffin replied with deliberate gravity, "is the odor
of holiness."

The question of whether children ought ever to attend divine
service still is debated week in and week out. It is a question that
should never come to any debate at all. The very concept of the
church as a family fellowship includes the youngest of that family. The meaning of infant Baptism (or in certain Churches the
dedication of children) implies their acceptance. Old-fashioned
proponents of the family pew, now supported by modern proponents also, declare that everyone of every age ought to be
present: "Old men, and babes, And loving friends and youths
and maidens gay!" as Coleridge phrased it. Nevertheless some
pastors object to the undisciplined voices of little ones; parents

33

become embarrassed by the stares of unsympathetic pewholders; and the fidgits of small fry frequently offend surrounding worshipers.

Some of the results of this intolerant attitude toward juvenile worshipers are quite unfortunate. Young parents may remain away from regular church worship for years on end until they get all their family started into older years. Some churches seeking a solution to the quandary have failed to find it in ersatz junior church services that segregate the young away from the church fellowship, or in child-care nurseries supervised by untrained volunteers who consider their semiannual turn at this duty an irksome burden.

A better solution is to be found in the family church service. To this service the entire family go together. Often it is held as the first or early service on Sunday, about 9:15 A.M. This worship of thirty to forty-five minutes is followed by church school classes for everyone — children and adults. Each element in the order of worship is so planned that some part of it is understandable by even the young members of the congregation; and the pastor makes frequent explanations concerning hymns, Scripture, the benediction, or other parts of the service. As usual in such instances, quite a number of adults inadvertently learn a few things they had not previously known. Hymns are carefully chosen from those also known in church school departments so that the nonreaders of the group can sing them from memory. And the same hymns are used for three or more successive weeks to familiarize families with them.

The sermonette is often given in the form of a story, intelligible to all the people present, although certain parts sometimes may be clearly identified for adults or for smaller children ("Now this is said especially for the mothers and fathers here . . ."). Many pastors make a habit of offering a children's sermon or story; and this can be done in good taste. However, it should be noted that as much care must be taken in the preparation of this feature as in the preparation of the sermon for an adult congregation, if it is to be done well and not to become a subject of ridicule. The sacrilege that has been committed in the guise of children's sermons delivered without preparation would be hard to gauge.

Even the adult sermon need not be above the heads of children in every detail. Jesus so often employed stories and illustrations so that the simplest of his hearers were not left out. Some preachers deliberately insert sections into their sermons that will appeal to younger minds in the congregation; and they call attention to them too. Preaching to the needs of children is not talking down to them. Sometimes their perception outdistances that of adults. We suspect that unsophisticated children's minds caught many points of Jesus' teaching that escaped their elders. The preacher who seeks to make his preaching relevant to family life will not want for material. The fact is that his congregation will suggest those topics on which they need help. Not a few ministers invite suggestions by means of a question box; and they find that children as well as adults ask for topics. In family worship services sermon topics can be organized to appeal to a congregation of many ages. The preacher who disciplines himself to make such sermons both understandable to the range of his hearers and brief enough to hold their attention will have made some marked strides in communicating to families. Some preachers keep attention through the use of continued stories, some with illustrated talks on Christian symbolism. In any case the pastor will have to work at the task of making his sermons apt for the family audience, for it is against a vast competition that he preaches. They are mindful of other influences that may outweigh the influence of his sermons. The life they live in their homes may completely deny the message of his preaching. As a result the families of the congregation may not be ready for his homiletics unless they are also helped to find a Christian dimension to their home life.

For his use of illustrations, the preacher will find a host of source material in literature. The stories that he reads to his own children are rich in such material: the various books of A. A. Milne for children, the classical tales from Hans Christian Andersen in the twenty-five-cent editions available at supermarkets, have a host of good material for illustrative purposes. On a dif-

ferent plane, *The Pilgrim's Progress* and especially the narratives
of the Bible are limitless in their possibilities. The one source
that the preacher must beware of using for illustrative material is
the lives of people he knows. Here he can do untold harm, even
if he disguises the cases, because the private lives of parishioners
and the confidences told him in an interview are not the stuff out
of which sermons can be constructed. It is actually the lazy
preacher who relies upon them. If he were reading and studying
as widely as he ought, he would find ample source material of a
safer nature in literature. One does not need to go beyond the
play *The Death of a Salesman* to find examples of immaturity,
or Willa Cather's story "Paul's Case" to locate misunderstanding
in family living. The novels of our day are frequently concerned
with family problems; and the characters often are psychological
cases in themselves. The risks attendant to citing actual cases
of living people are too well known to require detailing here.
The preacher may lose all his opportunity to be of help in counseling if the people feel that he preaches about them later on.
And if they recognize themselves in his sermon illustrations
(whether it is true or not), their fury can be boundless. Halford
Luccock tells of preaching in Atlantic City some years ago when
he cited the case of a woman's problem with her faith. It was a
fleeting, incidental section of his sermon, but at its close a
woman came up from the congregation and angrily accosted him
with: "How dare you discuss my cousin in Iowa in your sermon!" It is, to coin a phrase, a small world.

An order of worship for a family service might follow such a
liturgy as this:

> Opening Hymn of Praise
> Call to Worship
> Prayers of Invocation and Confession
> Hymn
> Responsive Reading or Scripture
> Pastoral Prayers or Litany
> Announcements
> Offering
> Anthem by the Youth Choir

Hymn (preschool children could leave after this hymn to go to their departments, if desired)

Sermonette Story

Closing Hymn (may be a recessional)

Benediction and Silent Prayer (with dismissal to all classes)

The values of such a plan are many: it allows the entire family to travel to church together; it is associated with a learning process that can be Christian education at its best; it has a direct and realistic link to family worship in the home; and it unites the entire family in the worship of God.

Family worship services have been gaining steadily during the past few years; and churches have found that they are richly adaptable to a number of emphases. So obvious is the need to teach children good habits of worship that it remains a mystery how it has been so long neglected. Protestant Episcopal churches have integrally linked the family service and their church school classes to provide an experience in family corporate worship, parents' classes, and children's classes.

Won't the attendance falter at the later adult service? some ask. Experience indicates that seldom does the later service suffer at all and that the family service attracts some people who had attended only occasionally before. One church that had had a slipping attendance instituted a second service for the family, and an officer ironically asked, " Does the rapid growth of our church demand a second service? " The pastor wisely replied that a store that does not have enough business should lengthen rather than reduce its hours. Family church services have grown so rapidly and healthily that in numerous parishes, they have now become the chief service of the week.

The scheduling, a consideration that looms large at the outset, is actually a minor detail once the official board has settled on the decision to have the family service. Some churches plan only occasional family services, substituting them for the usual weekly worship. Other churches prefer to set one Sunday per month as family day, and make this adaptation that day. Still others know the dual service schedule as an every-Sunday feature, usually placing the family service first. Some churches, compromising

between a permanent pattern and occasional services for the
family, may set a series of six successive Sundays for family
services, a plan that has merit but tends to be confusing for the
families.

The way that these family worship services are handled is as
variable as our denominations. In some Churches, of course, Holy
Communion is administered every week. Among these Churches,
the children often come forward to the altar rail with their parents to kneel and receive a blessing from the minister while the
adults receive the sacrament. The family service too is just the
time for such offices as the dedication of children or the sacrament of Baptism for infants. The whole church family is present
and the pastor has a marvelous opportunity to re-emphasize the
meaning of this rite. It is encouraging, moreover, to see the number of churches that now invite older brothers and sisters to stand
with their parents and the baby as one united family when the
Baptism takes place.

Special notice should be taken of the hymns sung during the
family service, that they be chosen wisely to be meaningful for
and singable by young children. It is wise indeed to repeat the
same hymn several weeks in succession so that it becomes thoroughly familiar. These same hymns, if taught in the church
school and suggested for worship in the home, become a part of
the family's hymn repertoire. It is difficult enough to achieve a
singing church without mystifying the youthful worshipers with
hymns that present inferior music, inconsistent theology, or un-
singable words. The practice of some churches to have the children leave the service for their extended sessions during the singing of a hymn is hardly calculated to help them respect Church
music. It is better by far for them to sing the hymn through to
its conclusion, and then to file out while the congregation remains standing and the organist plays a continuation.

Those who nostalgically yearn for the family pew are today
finding that it is with us again but with new meaning. The family worshiping together are helped to understand their faith
better as the pastor each week explains one part of the worship
and why it is included: this week the doxology, next week a

litany, and so forth. The great seasons of the Church year come into new importance to the minds of the congregation when they are highlighted as family festivals, rich with meaning for the home. The architecture of the church lives anew as the minister takes the time to introduce its symbolism to the young worshiper in a continuing attention Sunday after Sunday.

Many pastors also announce their sermon, text, Scripture, responsive readings, and hymns at least one week in advance so that families can use these same references for their weekday worship. Thus primary graders, just learning the skills of reading, can thereby prepare for a time of joy and participation in church rather than a period of frustration. This service has no reason to be less worshipful than the regular stated worship to which the church is accustomed; but the language ought to be more easily understood, and the total length briefer.

The obvious connection between the worship of the congregation and the family at worship in the home is somehow missed by many. But a great deal of the difficulty we have in convincing families that they ought to have a family altar stems from the unfavorable impression that they have of worship as a Christian practice at all. This link needs not only to be recognized but also to be utilized by an alert church that aids the one with the other. Worship begins with adults, and is fostered most effectively by parents. As James H. S. Bossard and Eleanor Boll noted in their *Ritual in Family Living,* rites do not endure where there is no adult pattern to nourish them.

Preaching About Family Concerns

Not only in the church service designated for families with small children but also in the service for adults, preaching is needed on family questions. Topics concerning relationships of marriage and parenthood are among the most popular here. Everyone seems to be acquainted with that frequently cited young pastor who felt it his duty each year to preach a sermon on how to bring up children. In his habit, the story goes, he persisted until he was married himself and had children. After that he never made that mistake again.

It's a cynical story in its way, and mistakenly it hangs the purpose of the sermon on the wrong peg. Instruction does play a part in preaching; but that is not preaching's primary purpose. The real concern of preaching is to proclaim God's Word with all of its good news: that God is reconciling the world unto himself, that with him there is forgiveness of sin. The preacher who sees his task in this light will not seek by any superior-to-thee pulpit stance to tell his pewholders how to have an upright family (they just may be doing a better job of it than the cleric), but rather will do something far more important by relating the good news of God to family living. The humble preacher can well identify with puzzled parents of his parish. Like Father Damien's classic sermon introduction to his leper congregation, "Fellow lepers," we can say with honest humility, "Fellow parents." In this approach is a healthy recognition that we have not surmounted all our problems, and that we share with our people the need for God's grace in family living.

The range of topics for sermons about the family is amazingly wide. One can preach on love and marriage, on the Christian interpretation of sex conduct, on parental responsibilities or filial responsibilities, on older people in the home, on in-law relationships, on facing family crisis on home relationships, on guilt, anxiety, and many more subjects. The National Council of Churches recently published a collection of such sermons as the project of their Joint Department of Family Life. Titles in that volume, *Sermons on Marriage and Family Life,* are illustrative: "Problems of Mixed Marriage," "Religion and the Home," "Will Your Marriage Be Christian?", "You Shall Not Commit Adultery," and others. For many years, Theodore Adams, pastor of the First Baptist Church of Richmond, Virginia, has built a reputation for preaching about marriage. His collection of sermons, *Making Your Marriage Succeed,* serves as a commendable guide in this field, for Dr. Adams has blended Christian theology, common sense, and humor into a type of preaching that is easy to listen to and at the same time is remarkably helpful. Dr. A. W. Beaven, well-known dean of the Colgate Rochester Divinity School, has made a specialty also of preaching on family life, and has shown a gift for choosing the apt subject: "Look Before You Leap," "Does Flaming Youth Mean Burnt Out Homes?", "Whom God Hath (Not) Joined Together," "The Family Altar and the Altered Family" (cited in Beaven's *The Fine Art of Living Together*).

The touchiest of these topics for most preachers are those which deal with sexual relations. It is difficult to deal as frankly with this field as the Bible does. But the Bible is our guide. The preacher who seeks Biblical guidance on this field will find it in large quantities. A few examples would suffice. Concerning sex conduct, Col. 3:5-15, II Tim. 3:1-7, Rom. 1:24-32, and Titus, ch. 2, are among the many passages on which expository sermons can be based. Marriage receives its attention in the Scriptures: Gen., chs. 1 and 2, Heb., ch. 13, John, ch. 2, and numerous other passages. Those sermons that lift us above our poor average of living and help us to see the glorious gift of family life where God's grace can work so effectively: such are a major part of our family ministry.

Family Worship and Christian Commitment

It is doubtful whether a family church service can long continue unless it is fed by means of family worship in the home. But family worship proves to be one of the knottiest problems that confronts us. Proffered solutions range all the way from an idyllic desire to recapitulate the pattern of "The Cotter's Saturday Night" in downtown Milwaukee to the warning of Regina H. Westcott in *The Family Lives Its Religion* that no child should be exposed to family prayers until he has had the freedom and the time to think through his position about the existence of God. These two "solutions" are equally objectionable.

The real issue, of course, lies in the Christian commitment of the family. Once this is established, family worship falls into place just as does the Christian teaching in the home. Only gradually do families learn for themselves that the doctrine of justification by faith also applies directly to them. Some of them make valiant attempts to build a Christian family, straining hard to accomplish all the "right things," set rituals of worship, set standards of stewardship, and set ways of relationships as if somehow they have to attain perfection. But theirs is a false theology. They try too hard to do the impossible. A firm reliance upon the grace of God provides a Christian aura for the home far more effectively than all their efforts in good works. The simple truth is that families need God.

Families are frequently admonished by the church to hold worship in their homes. Yet the pattern for home worship that the churches usually suggest is little different from that of several generations ago when farm families gathered by the wood-burning stove in the kitchen to "hear a chapter and have prayers." What is self-evident to young families must also permeate church leadership: that the type of family worship that once fitted into a farm family's morning after milking chores is not nearly so useful for the 1950's. Today's families do not worship as their forebears did because they don't live as they lived.

For one thing, most current worship materials published for families err at two extremes: either the materials are written with such a juvenile style that the parents become mere spectators while children worship; or else they are constructed so obviously for adults that the children are unable to appreciate more than a fraction of the content. Apologists for the first type insist that adults can worship on a juvenile level when they get down to where the children live; apologists for the other subscribe to the "let them grow into it" school that believes someday they'll understand. To be fair, there is some justice in both these claims. Yet they lose sight of the fact that unless the whole family, adults and children alike, gain a reality feeling in their worship, for some it is going to remain mere form.

Surely the clue is on the emotional, rather than the intellectual, level. However much children and parents differ physically and mentally, it can be ruefully acknowledged that they are much alike emotionally. In this realm, where the generations are not far apart, together they can learn to rely upon the grace of God in family living. When finally materials are published that take cognizance of this fact, entire families will again be led into the presence of God. The way is already pointed by some of our most successful, though still incomplete insights. The home worship service of tomorrow will be prepared by parents for twentieth century families rather than for the rural family of a hundred years ago. They will be brief, for modern homes are hurried and all the sermons about taking sufficient time for God will not alter bus schedules or school bells. We have it on high authority that God hardly answers prayer for our much speaking anyway. It is possible for families to worship in shifts just as work is done in shifts. One section of the family may find that their best time to worship is in the evening, and another at the breakfast table. While it is certainly preferable for the whole family group to be together for this event, it need not be given up if some members follow an irregular workaday schedule. Moreover, as retreatants well know, it is feasible during a meal to listen even while eating as someone reads the Bible or a devotional classic. Such a practice, long known to the monastics, has value that carries over into the busy life of modern families.

Training Families to Worship

Pastors who have been able personally to train their families in family worship report immense gains in spiritual awareness for the entire parish. Richard Baxter, the great English hymn writer, was able to revive a cold and nearly empty church by visiting from home to home in that parish and instituting family worship wherever he stopped. Today there are up-to-date Richard Baxters who call upon their parishioners with worship materials, projectors, and film slides on worship, and their own example in leadership. We owe it to our people to teach them the way in family worship, for the kind of leadership they get makes a more profound impression and is more motivating than the quality of literature used. In his leadership of the family, the pastor will do well to recall that this is not a miniature church service, but another kind of experience, home centered, and home grown. Worship in the home should be different from the formal service of Sunday, for it needs to be open to spontaneity and ever ready for new adaptations.

Some Special Means of Training for Family Worship

1. Family nights at church likewise prove to be ideal training events for family worship. This old system, now enjoying a new vogue, brings together church families for an occasional meal and a program; and these programs are as variable as the needs of the parish. Often, however, they provide an opportunity for demonstration in family worship. Films on this subject are exhibited. The families discuss the ways and means of worship in their homes; and one family can lead the others in worship that night, not as a mere display of technique, but as a means of directing their praise toward God at a family night program. This is educational; but it is also true worship.

2. Daily vacation church schools, now more than half a century old in American churches, have taken a new twist these latter years when their enrollment has been comprised of families rather than boys and girls exclusively. Both the parents and their children are registered in study classes and activities; and this schedule, while it permits fewer sessions, increases the effectiveness of the school. Having the parents present as well as the children makes possible a learning experience not previously imagined. It can hardly be a surprise then that learning to worship in the home has resulted from this new plan. When the entire family is present in this educational experience, instruction in family worship becomes one of the foremost subjects and one of the most successful.

3. Family camping, rapidly growing in popularity all across the land, offers our most concentrated single experience to educate entire families together in Christian living. This is possible through a well-organized summer experience, and upon occasion also at other times of the year. The justification for the Church to engage in family camping is that it advances the main evangelistic and educational task of the Church within the basic unit of social living, the home. When the church family camp falls short of this purpose, it no longer has any excuse for being a part of the Christian education enterprise. Family camping aims to aid families in their Christian living, and to help them to transfer back to their homes the insights and techniques they gain. Thus

emphasis is laid upon family worship to the end that these families will still be worshiping when they again get into their routine world at home. Still, it would be an unsatisfactory experience if all the interest were to be put in terms of the future carry-away aspects of the program. The fact is that this experience in joyous Christian living is of tremendous value for what happens right there. Transfer values are added as a large and appreciated bonus.

Needless to say, the leadership for family camping is different from that for other camping. In one manner of speaking, it requires a smaller staff than other camps. In another way, this type of camping has far and away the heaviest concentration of leadership of any type. The variable factor here, of course, is to be found in the parents. Obviously they are the real counselors in this kind of camp, each pair responsible for one unit of the camp family — their own family. Qualified or not, our family camp counselors come to us ready-made, and their training for this special task must be in-service training. Without fail, their period of in-service training proves of value and aids them in their worship as a family group.

4. Each year in May, National Family Week is highlighted as the churches of America together emphasize the need for Christian family education and their consciousness of the importance of the family. The main emphasis of the week always is placed upon the need for families to acknowledge their dependence upon God in worship. As a result, special worship materials, " Pages of Power," are published by the National Council of Churches; and many denominations and parishes lift the theme of the week to assist families in their plans to worship. Because of this annual program, some families who begin to worship together for the first time continue to do so as a habit. When the departments and classes of the church follow through this worship emphasis in National Family Week, and co-ordinate it with the entire educational program, homes cannot help being challenged by the suggestion.

Begin Early and Persevere

Deep in the fastness of the Pocono Mountains a honeymoon
lodge puts printed table graces in the dining room for its starry-
eyed patrons. The management reports that this is one of the
most popular features of its service, because most young newly-
weds seem to be searching for helps in religious ritual for their
new homes. As is suggested in Chapter 5 of this book, premarital
counseling ought also to include instruction in family worship
so that a new family begins well. In a master's dissertation at San
Francisco Theological Seminary, Shirley S. Jennings surveyed
patterns of family worship in lay homes. It was her discovery that
of those who practiced family worship the largest group had
begun during honeymoon days, and the second largest when
their children were old enough to participate. Only a few had
taken up worship in the home after any considerable years of
marriage. An early beginning is important. Significantly, some
of our finest educational opportunities occur before a child ever
reaches school age; and those children who are brought up in an
atmosphere of family worship very nearly learn to pray before
they can actually talk. In this connection we are reminded by
Randolph Crump Miller in *The Clue to Christian Education* that
to small children their parents *are* the church for a considerable
period in their early life. To such children family worship can
always be a real experience, of personal import to them. The
family that allow every individual to get into the act of worship,
and introduce new forms or ideas gradually enough for everyone to understand, will encounter little resistance. But if they
attempt in some fashion woodenly to follow a set pattern, and
fail to account for the actual needs of their family, the practice
may well falter and fail.

It is to be expected, however, that there will come periods of
restlessness and spiritual listlessness. Even the saints have testi-
fied to dry seasons of the soul when they could not feel the presence of God. Families of today that are not saintly by nature,
nor patient in well-doing, are certain to reach a point of liturgical
fatigue. What then follows makes a vast difference to the church.
For if they allow these uninspirational times to dominate their

feeling toward the practice of worship, family worship will not long endure. But if they can be encouraged to persevere even when the experience seems routine, the nearness of God will again be apparent and a realization of the worth of this act will grow upon them not because they had done it to get some subjective value from it, but because they were worshiping God as an act of love and praise.

Some concepts in our readings and in our prayers turn out to be old ideas for younger minds, too mature for the children to grasp or completely to understand. That some profound spiritual insights are also beyond adults must be admitted also. But difficult concepts can be translated into more common currency that enables us all to grasp them at least in part. Bible readings, for instance, can be chosen from a variety of translations; and that pastor who introduces his families to the modern translations of the Scriptures does them a favor. Indeed the pastor's own reading of Scripture in the church service will have a noticeable effect upon the homes of his people. If the Bible is read as if it is not meant to be understood, in a manner that seems to indicate that this is pretty dull stuff, an obscure rite whose origins are lost in meaninglessness and history, then family worship will also suffer. But if the pastor can give guidance to his people in the selection of readings, the use of modern translations, and the ways that these can be explained or paraphrased, he will have passed on good training.

Not only through visitation, but also in the church school, and through fellowship and especially in the stated services of the church meetings, families can be taught to worship. Special seasons and circumstances open the way to worship in the home, and ought not to be neglected. Some families never learn to pray together until taught by the pastor to do so in time of illness or of death. Others, however, learn without so great a crisis. Thanksgiving, Easter, Christmas are occasions that lead naturally to worship. For these holidays, many churches distribute materials that families can use for worship. The practice of supplying an Advent wreath for the Advent season and lighting a candle for each Sunday of that forward-looking time leads many families into worship. The wreath, fashioned out of green boughs, and surmounted with four white candles, is all aglow for the final service just before Christmas. In recent years, not only churches but even greeting card companies have been distributing prayers and lections for this season's worship.

Christmas often moves families to worship who have not habitually worshiped in their homes. It is singularly appropriate for the pastor to send a Christmas greeting to his people that includes a Christmas worship service for the home. Families who have never gathered together for family worship before sometimes begin the tradition from this greeting. A pastor either may purchase one of the cards merchandised for the purpose or may compose one himself. Such a card can include the traditional Christmas lections, a poem or a hymn, perhaps a brief message and prayers. A litany composed for such a Christmas family service follows:

LEADER: O God, whose love for our world is so great that no gift has been too precious to give us, no sacrifice too large:
FAMILY: *We give thee thanks, O God.*
LEADER: For the gift of thy Son, our Lord Jesus Christ, and all that his life has meant to us:
FAMILY: *We give thee thanks, O God.*
LEADER: For the light that overcomes darkness, for love that dispels hate, for hope that casts out fear:
FAMILY: *We give thee thanks, O God.*
LEADER: For the spirit of generosity in Christmas, for the strengthening of family ties, and for the joy we know at this season:
FAMILY: *We give thee thanks, O God.*
LEADER: As once more we read the marvelous story of thy Word in the flesh of Jesus, and we hear again of his coming to teach the good news that the lost can be saved and peace will yet rule men's hearts, we lift to thee our hearty praise:
FAMILY: *We give thee thanks, O God. Amen.*

In the Protestant Reformation, the family at worship was spotlighted as a new departure. It was at the hearthside that little children learned the true meaning of the priesthood of all believers. It was at their mothers' knees that they began to understand something of the sovereignty of God. Both Martin Luther and John Calvin left a profound impression upon the worshiping families of their time; and there is good reason to believe that their influence here at times outweighed their influence either in theology or in politics, great as this was. Their concentration upon the family as a little church caused the center for prayers to shift for a while from the nave to the hearth. " Every family," E. Rosenstock-Huessy reports, " now was cemented into a spiritual unit while before it was purely hereditary and economic. By the reading of Scripture, by the singing of hymns, and the common prayer at meals in the native tongue in the homes of lay families, their faith gained a new power." (*The Christian Future*, p. 46.) For that day as for this, when the family truly worshiped together, it was actually the Church at worship in that home.

The family altar may not evangelize the world in this generation, but it could go a long way toward opening church families to a deeper practice of Christianity. And the pastor who promotes worship in the homes as he makes his calls and helps to meet the needs of his people aids this deepening process. The thinking, if it could be called that, that has allowed this practice to fall into neglect is the type that supposes the church exists only in a brick building at the corner of Washington Street and Central Avenue. So long as we keep a parochial concept of the church and fail to note that our church is most profound when it is *ecclesia domestica,* the house church, our worship will be pew-bound. When, however, pastors and people break out of this confining concept and see the family for what it is, " the Church in thy house," then materials will improve, training in worship will increase, and prayer at home will be as common as it now is unusual.

In a bit of whimsical yet solid philosophizing, John Oliver Nelson has said:

"Granted, material things do so dominate us today that perhaps only as we see the chalice on our mantel or the holy paten beside the refrigerator shall we say, 'Surely the Lord is in this place,' Then too in a time of specialization, it may be scandal for anyone but a duly ordained person to preach and pray and assure us of the Presence.

"Might not our knowing children themselves whisper that, after all, Father is not a priest, Mother not trained to explain Scripture, our Early American dinette suite after all not a real altar.

"Ah, but 'the family altar' never did look like an altar: it was a plain table! Father as leader of worship never did wear a stole; he was just a Christian parent. Mother never did quite get straight the 'cansts' and 'thous' of prayer, and never heard of the documentary hypothesis about the Old Testament: she was merely a prayerful person who knew she was dealing with the Word.

"It does take 'a heap o' livin'' to make a house a church, but it is being done in many thousands of households. Even as we build elaborately to give the Lord a house down the street, is not our highest concern to keep 'church' from ever getting out of 'house'?" (*Kirkridge Contour*, June, 1956.)

3

THE PASTORAL CARE
OF CHURCH FAMILIES

*We are handicapped on all sides but we
are never frustrated: we are puzzled, but
never in despair. We are persecuted, but
we never have to stand it alone: we may
be knocked down but we are never knocked out!*
— II Cor. 4:8, 9 (Phillips' Translation).

More time is wasted in pastoral calling than in any other pastoral
function. The purposeless, meaningless social visit of duty, simply
to fulfill some standard to " get around to the membership once
a year " can hardly be justified for whatever values are claimed
for it. True, in a merely social call, the pastor may happen in on
a situation that requires his help, but it is a haphazard, expensive way to provide pastoral care. Parish families may appreciate
the friendly "hello" of their minister, or they may even expect
him to stop by regularly; but such social niceties can be superficial and without value either to the fellowship or to the family's
welfare.

The alarming incidence of breakdowns among clergymen,
which has been receiving attention from several quarters of late,
is not unrelated to the busy, enervating calling schedule of the
conscientious (albeit sometimes un-co-ordinated) pastor. To make
scores of calls each week can take so much out of the already
burdened prebendary that unless they are carefully planned for a
known purpose, they hardly justify the time they cost.

Yet few other functions in the pastor's job description can be
so rewarding as calling upon families in the parish. There is no

substitute for what George Buttrick has dubbed "consecrated shoe leather." To be in the homes of his people at times of great emotional importance is a pastor's privilege. Many a physician or social case worker can well envy his passport into the homes of church families.

Every week the pastor finds himself close to some family at a time of high importance, of crisis, or of significance to their lives. He comes to them at times of great happiness as well as sorrow. The alert pastor is there with premarital guidance when marriage is contemplated, when the baby is born and when the baby is baptized into the Church. He knows when separation occurs, such as when young people leave for college, for military service, or for employment in distant cities. He is with his families in time of sickness, accident, and death. He is often in their homes at times of anniversaries, or honors, or dedications. And he is there again when sweeping sudden loss has occurred, when crises arrive that are too difficult to cope with, or when guilt and shame have overcome them.

On all these occasions, happy or unhappy, our people are more aware of their need for counsel and more ready to receive it than at any other time. They may not have the courage to come (in fact, they may even feel that their pastor would not approve of them in light of some new circumstance); but they will usually be open to your ministrations if you but let them know that you do care how they are faring in these times of significant events in the home.

Taking the initiative in calling at a time when congratulations are in order is easy enough. Taking the initiative when some soul-searing crisis has occurred is far different, requiring unusual tact and understanding. This was illustrated in the case of one pastor who learned that a church member's daughter was in serious trouble. He went to visit the family and talked with them; but they could not bring themselves to mention the problem. The pastor called again and again in that home, and the daughter's difficulty was never mentioned until many months later. Then it was that her father said: " I couldn't talk to you about it. I knew that you knew, and that you were my friend in those dark days. That was what mattered." Such empathy can reach deeper than verbal conversation about a problem; it gets down to the feeling level where we all live.

Toward More Efficient Calling

Complete parish records are important beyond description; and an adequate family record is imperative. To go on a family call with full knowledge of the size and nature of the family is to be prepared to be of service. The pastor should certainly know who the members of the family are, when they were last visited, and the participation of each in the church program. Not to know their names is inexcusable, and seems to communicate to the family that this clerical caller cares little about them as people. A 4″ x 6″ index card on each family, or a Keysort file of perforated cards, makes possible an accurate family record and vastly increases the effectiveness of parish calling.

Today's pastor keeps a schedule so packed with events that he must be ever watchful for ways to improve his time. It will save him many hours, and increase the satisfaction of calls, if he telephones ahead for an appointment. Pastors who follow this practice report that the entire family manages to be present, and that it opens the way to speak of more essential items than the weather, to talk of the minister's role, and the church fellowship. In such a setting, already expectant, it is altogether natural to read from the Bible and to offer family prayer. This indeed can be a reminder of family worship in some homes; and it prepares the way for a close pastoral relationship to families. It is not enough that families repair to church for times of conventional rites and services, where they are challenged by the proclamation of the Word, where their children are baptized, where the young folks are married, and where there are services for the dead. If the Church is to have a godly impact upon the homes of its people, it will be necessary to do nothing less than introduce Christ into family life.

For nothing is truer than this — there cannot be a Christian family life unless all relationships reflect a family's relationship to Christ. No ritual, no frequency of family prayers, no record of church attendance alone will make a family Christian. The grace of God in Christ transforms home life and makes it Christlike; but nothing else will. To this truth the pastor testifies as he comes into the family circle and gathers them in prayer.

As the post office has zoned off its delivery routes, churches have likewise subdivided the parish into zones for more efficient administration and ministry. The pastor who makes his family appointments according to zone saves both steps and time. Moreover, this suggests natural neighborhood groups for parent meetings, or even for group-calling on three or four families gathered for an evening in some one home. This system lends itself to lay visitation. Trained callers such as deacons who are assigned responsibility for one area can assist by visiting church homes and cover certain zones. Thus active families can be asked to visit inactive or new families — and they often make more impact than the minister can. Trained lay callers can be educated to sense when something in the home is amiss, and notify the pastor of illness or difficulty. They can also show newcomers a genuine welcome to the community in a less " professional manner " than the clergyman. Whether we like it or not, our first pastoral visits to new residents will be regarded, at least in part, as a duty. The friendly call of a neighbor is more folksy.

The pastor who needs an opening for his call always has an easy wedge into conversation if he brings something in hand. Religious literature can be delivered to families in just this way. One West Coast pastor, newly called to his church, loaded up his automobile with samples of all the church curriculum materials and went forth to the homes of his people. He delivered copies to each and every home in the membership, and thereby got acquainted in a splendid way. The delivery of the teacher-parent magazines, and an explanation concerning their use, provided a workable plan for his visitation and a purposeful call.

The family call is an opportunity to explain the program of the church, relating the children to the church school and encouraging family participation in curriculum, worship, and stewardship. Pastoral calling reaches a high level when organized around the welfare of the family. Calling on parents in behalf of the church school and its children has become generally accepted in recent years. This task can be shared by minister and lay leaders who are well briefed in the church school program. This type of home visitation, however, has relevance only when the parents have some understanding of their role in the Christian training of their children. Merely to offer guidance materials, such as books and quarterly magazines, is virtually without meaning unless fathers and mothers gain some intimation of how these resources can help them!

When, therefore, the pastor calls in the home on behalf of the church school to inquire about an absence or to explain the church program he must first know the relevance of Christian education for parents as well as for teachers. Parents need also to come into a new understanding of the will of God, who has placed in their hands the privilege of rearing children. This important assignment is a holy charge; and most parents realize something, however slightly, of this truth. To this truth the pastor testifies in a purposeful call in the home. He can make reference to the immense influence that the parents have upon their children, genuinely complimenting the father and mother upon their contribution to their youngsters' lives. It can be acknowledged that the church school is unable to take on the complete Christian education of the children entrusted to it but can only serve as an additional resource to the home which really does the most powerful religious teaching. It is advisable to clarify how the church school program assists parents in this responsibility they have. If there is a class for parents, or an adult study group, or a parents association, this is the place to urge their participation. In a family call, the pastor shows interest not only in the children but also in the parents.

It is not wise for the pastor or caller to do all the talking. He should listen too. Parents can be counted on to be at least as interested in their children as the church teachers and officials who may call on them! Their comments ought also to be heard with interest and patience; but it is astonishing how many clergymen understand their calls in terms of delivering little homilies to apt listeners.

Family Evangelism

Brother Lawrence, it will be remembered, had a famous and commendable habit in prayer. He would shoot swift, brief petitions or intercessions to God on any occasion, without stopping his work for a moment. In such a fashion the pastor also pursues his full day's work, and he can offer a sentence of prayer as he approaches the door of a household in visitation. This is a prayer that the call will serve God's will, and that through it we might minister satisfactorily in his name. Ministering to families is a holy work, and this part of our evangelistic mission always needs to be approached prayerfully.

Time was when faith was interpreted as so personal a matter that evangelism had reference only to an individual. " Win them one by one " was the theme song of that day. Gradually, however, it became apparent that this exclusive connotation of the term " evangelism " did an injustice to families. Just as the Philippian jailer was converted to Christianity together with his entire family, much of our present-day evangelistic effort has also become family-centered.

So important is this to some churches that they show a marked reluctance to receive into their membership lone individuals apart from their family members. This is based on sound experience. Too often one person has a strong religious concern not shared by others in his home, and after a long time his enthusiasm can wane through the cold indifference of husband, sister, or mother. Many times a young person comes back from a summer conference with the thrill of inspiration only to have a parent or brother pour cold water on this " passing phase."

Because the family is bound together by blood ties and intimate relationship, it is highly desirable that evangelistic calling take into consideration the entire household. The calling that precedes a reception of members into the church can be made upon the entire family gathered together in the home, with everyone present. To be members of one church is consistent with living in the same home. Many divided families, e.g., mixed marriages, can get along somehow, but there is greater warmth in religious interest when the entire family can share it.

But some families seem compelled to be split on the issue of religious faith. Some are interested, other members are antagonistic. In such a spot, of course, the church gladly welcomes those who will come. In cases of parental indifference to the religious training of their children, the church must aid parents to assume their responsibility and encourage them in it, yet meanwhile make up for their deficiency. For these, indeed, the church can sometimes provide the larger family fellowship that is needed in the faith. There is a system, related in H. A. Hamilton's little book *The Family Church,* among the Congregational churches of England whereby carefully selected and trained adults sponsor children whose parents show no interest in the church. These sponsors stand with the children at Baptism, guide them in their church life, sitting with them during worship, getting them to church school, helping them as spiritual counselors. Both the parents and the children are first visited and prepared for the experience. Although it is not the primary purpose of the sponsor system, the parents have sometimes been led to take a greater interest in the church that has shown so great an interest in their children.

Visitation of unchurched families is not the project of one church alone. It is one of those shared responsibilities which a council of churches or a community can do together, such as taking a community religious census, or conducting a community family life clinic as administered by the National Council of Churches, or a group of churches of the same denomination co-operating in a visitation upon the area's unchurched. In co-operative Protestantism one feature of courtesy and good administration is regularly observed: where a family is discovered to be part of another Church tradition, their name and address is referred to the appropriate pastor.

Unto Us a Child Is Born

Knowing the profound nature of the experience of birth in any family, the pastor stays close to a couple when their child is born. The writer will never forget one couple who had fervently wanted a child for some years. They hoped and prayed; and as their pastor I also shared in these hopes and prayers. At long last, in God's good time a baby was born. The young father that morning rushed into the church study and announced that his wife had just given birth to their first child, a realization of hope after many years of marriage. His heart was full, and his tongue was tied. " I don't know how to say it; you say it for me," he requested; and there the two of us knelt and prayed in thanksgiving for the new life that God had given. The profundity of the birth experience affects everyone. This God-given life is at once something from him, and something of ourselves. We are awed by it; we can appropriately be speechless before it.

Something of the wonder of the parent is captured in the words of Fritz Künkel in his *What Do You Advise?* (p. 259): " The birth of a baby is not merely a physical phenomenon. In every parent as he looks on his child for the first time, a kind of birth takes place too: a rebirth into deeper social responsibility and higher consciousness. The new life within the parent must keep pace with the growth of the child."

Yet not every so-called blessed event is blessed. Some parents hold out no welcome to the new life. Perhaps he comes to a family unready for his arrival, or he may arrive to drive a wedge between husband and wife who had no realization how this little intruder would affect their own relationship. Some people resemble Gestas in John Oxenham's *Cross Roads,* who said that he would not walk a mile to see any baby that was ever born because he had one at home that cried night and day. The pastor's task here is one of reconciliation. In such rejection can be the root of incalculable future trouble. The church has to help these parents accept their child so that he can accept himself. An unwanted child can be a curse not only to the parents who are embittered at his arrival, but to himself; for he carries in his very being the making of his own neuroses. Never understanding why his parents reject him, he grows up emotionally stunted for want of the very love that is essential to his development. For such a problem, pastoral counseling will probably be inadequate, especially because it may not be permitted. But group therapy can be of untold aid; and this is the genius of the church fellowship, that it often comprises group therapy in motion. The churches that have formed couples clubs composed of expectant parents provide a fellowship that meets for study during the months preceding the arrival of the babies. After the babies come, these same parents continue together as a fellowship group. Such a plan goes far in alleviating the confusion of the parents for whom another baby has not been a "blessed event." A marvelously teachable time for parents is that period of infanticipation. Parentcraft classes offered by church councils and community agencies are of great assistance to young men and women who need assurance and understanding about birth and babyhood. One church has a "Stork Club" that brings expectant parents together for movie discussions about birth and babyhood, for an acquaintance with the literature on the subject and a time of sharing. But this is not all. This is also the best place for preparation in Christian parenthood, of that depth which receives a partnership with God for the training of the child "in the nurture and admonition of the Lord." To learn something of their God-ordained role in parenthood and to comprehend the divine nature of this gift is at least as important as a class in learning the Read method of childbirth, or the way to change a diaper.

Since 1939 the American birth rate has been climbing steadily, and the busy pastor finds it necessary to pay more attention to the phase of his ministry that welcomes new lives into the parish and into the world. Some pastors wait out the anxious period at the hospital with the father, or walk the floor with him. Some plan to get there the first day after the baby has been born to visit with the mother and offer a thanksgiving prayer. Some have a church visitor or a calling committee who assist in this important ministry. These visitors in some churches have worked out a routine of delivering flowers, gifts from the church, and family worship literature. The Sunday morning church service can recognize the arrival of a new baby in the parish by a simple announcement in the bulletin or from the pulpit.

Whether the church sends a gift to the mother or child or has a packet of appropriate teaching materials ready for the young parents is a matter for local preference and custom. Normal

office routine, however, should care for two details: entering the
child's name on the nursery roll and making suitable arrangements for baptism at an early date. The pastor should see that
the nursery roll supervisor or that the committee on family life
takes care of the nursery roll. In these days of rising birth rate,
this is an active job. The child remains on the nursery roll until
he is old enough to enter into the activities of the nursery department, usually at about age three. Until that time he can be remembered with greetings each year on his birthday, which can
also be an occasion for relating to the parents and the whole
family some of the deeply believed doctrines of the Church
concerning its children.

It is one of the good fortunes of our day that maternal and
infant mortality rates have dropped so low as to make death at
delivery quite an unusual occurrence. The birth of a baby no
longer presents the great crisis that it once did. Still, it is a time
filled with thrilling events, and the church should be there. Calling upon mothers with new babies is a part of the family ministry that ought never to be omitted. Mothers at this time may
feel the presence of God in a new way that they have never known
before. A father may be filled with a gladness that the dispensing
of cigars can never express. The birth of a child in the parish is
a time for rejoicing as well as for instruction. There is a valuable
service in *The Book of Common Prayer* known as " the Church-
ing of Women," a thanksgiving service following childbirth. It
collects our feelings of awe and of gratitude and expresses them
in one of life's most profound mysteries, a mystery that is acknowledged when we present the child before God in the sacrament of Baptism.

The Baptism of Children

In those delightful descriptions of " life with father," Clarence
Day assures us that his forthright sire had a vigorous opinion
about every topic. This was certainly no less true of Baptism.
Baptism, insisted Mr. Day, was nothing but a lot of prayers, a
mere technicality, and an impracticable rigamarole.

Such thinking might be dismissed as the ridiculous heresy of a fictionalized biography were it not for the haunting notion that this just might represent the general attitude of many other people, among them even some churchmen. Question any congregation, and you will soon locate considerable confusion about the sacrament of Baptism. Few parishioners can recall ever having heard a sermon on the subject. Many have only the haziest notions of its purpose. Not a few generously mix together false impressions gleaned from other faiths and peculiar sacrilegious customs with the Christian doctrine. This discussion is within the Reformed view, wherein the author stands. Some readers will have a different orientation, but the implications for ministry to families are much the same.

It is surprising how widespread is the erroneous notion that the baptizing of a baby contains some kind of magic. As if a child would now be luckier, healthier, or holier, some parents (or grandparents or neighbors) tremble until the ceremony is safely over. Much of this superstition, of course, comes from the mistaken belief that if the child were to die before being baptized, he would remain unsaved. The Reformed tradition has never included this superstition, and there is no basis for it in the Bible, or in the mainstream of Christian theology. The love of Almighty God is too great, too merciful, to be funneled through the liturgy of the sacrament of Baptism.

Less somber but no less mistaken is the pious hope that the baptized child will be somehow better behaved than he was prior to the service. Thus a despairing grandmother could challenge the mischievous young William Saroyan following his baptism: "You are now baptized. Do you feel any better?" Brash indeed would be that pastor who held out any promise that Baptism makes a child feel better, becomes less irritable, or makes him easier to control.

Another unwarranted idea associated with infant Baptism is that the sacrament is but a charming social affair. Those who hold this view generally speak of it as "christening" and look forward to the festivities that usually follow after the guest of honor has been put to bed. What we have here are the vestiges of the ancient ceremony in which a baby first officially received his name. But today when babies are brought to Baptism, their names are already registered on a birth certificate, and, technically speaking, christening as such is unnecessary.

Nor is infant Baptism what the uninstructed may come to suppose it to be — a mere empty ritual. Some assume it to be one of those quaint, agreeable habits of the Church to which they have become accustomed as a harmless and unessential rite. There is nothing in this view that prevents it from going to the extreme reported from the mission field some years back when an enthusiastic Chinese general converted his troops by command and had them all baptized at once with a hose. Quite apart from such exaggerated action, the attitude that overemphasizes the ritual aspects of Baptism unfortunately detracts from the subsequent obligations of parents to fulfill their solemn vows.

Pastors sometimes treat this high occasion with a carelessness that is inexcusable, and this may well be the reason that parishioners take it lightly. Failing to take full cognizance of the continuing significance of Baptism, and the ongoing relationships involved for church and family, the service is often held in grand isolation. At its worst, the Baptism service is just that — an isolated experience unrelated to family life. It is as if the parson were to drop into the Amazon jungle by helicopter, sprinkle a baby, and fly away again, nevermore to return. The Baptism service, however, is realistic about family life. It is implicitly acknowledged that this child will be in the affectionate protection and care of the parents for a very long time when he is not directly accessible to the church at all.

To the minister the sacrament of infant Baptism is a challenge in education. The church family must be instructed in the nature of this sacrament. That it is a solemn covenant offered by God to his people and serves as a divine initiation rite into Christ's Church must be clearly communicated to church people if they are to overcome the notion that Baptism remains an event of passing charm and minor importance. Churches of all denominations have begun to systematize their Baptism education so that this once neglected doctrine is better explained. In one church, for instance, the pastor organizes a fellowship group of parents who are looking forward to the baptism of their children. In an evening or two of sharing together with the pastor, they are given a chance to get acquainted, have a description of the doctrine of Baptism as well as the mechanics of the service (it even allays some fears if the pastor frankly tells them that he uses warm water so that the child will not be shocked into a cry), see a strip film about Baptism, and participate in a question period. This evening session goes a long way toward helping parents to understand the sacrament, and often opens up opportunities for counseling with the parents. Their faith too is involved. Unless they can believe and practice this religion themselves, their children have scant opportunity to witness Christianity for years.

Infant Baptism, as practiced in the Reformed tradition, has far-reaching implication for the Christian family. Parents are invited to share in the sacred covenant between God and themselves. They agree to uphold their end as parents and carry through their pledge to rear their children " in the nurture and admonition of the Lord." It is our faith that in making it possible for us to have children, God on his part has endowed each new life with an all-important birthright, which is the privilege of a place in the family of God's own people. That this birthright is often accepted or rejected in the early years of life reveals how influential is the training a child receives in the home. That is why such considerable stress is put upon the parents' own faith, and why they are called upon to confess that faith and, if need be, to renew it.

In certain Protestant traditions this sacrament also marks the reception of a new member into Christ's church. From this time on, he is accounted one of the baptized members of a redeeming fellowship. Jesus called little children to him, saying that the Kingdom of God belonged to such. Paul, interpreting the mind of Christ, gave assurance that the children of believers are to be counted among the church family. When the child has come to the place where he can make rational decisions of his own, he will be given opportunity to confirm the vows parents make for him and to enter into communicant membership of the church.

Even at baptism, however, the child, along with other children, is a part of the church. He is entitled to all the blessings this implies: guidance and discipline of the church and its ministry, training in the education of the church school, the prayers of the congregation, and the security that results from a sense of belonging to the fellowship. But being part of a church implies more than rights and privileges. It implies duties, and these he will learn from observing his parents. The measure of his loyalty will be influenced largely by them. As a child of the covenant, he was born into the household of God; but it is the parents' responsibility to see that he remains within it and grows there.

In a similar way the church also assumes a sacred duty in the service of Baptism. The Christian congregation is the true sponsor of the child; and as the members receive him into their midst with the administration of the sacrament, they are obligated with God's help to aid in this task of Christian nurture. They too are concerned that he shall come to the place where he will make the decision to profess his own faith in Christ as his Lord and Saviour. To this end, the church provides a Sunday church school, with its teaching staff and curriculum; Christian activities and opportunities of service for children and youth; regular occasions for worship; and a fellowship with believers whose faith and life can be a source of inspiration and strength to each child of the church family. Christian upbringing is first of all the work of the home. But the church can and does provide leadership and materials to help in shouldering this task.

Baptism begins and ends as an act of God, God calling his people to enter into a vital relationship with him. Those who are given responsibility for the nursery roll and those officers who arrange baptisms for the church must be carefully instructed in the doctrine of Christian Baptism lest they cancel out the teachings of the Church by their own misunderstanding. The child as a token of the love between wife and husband is placed in the hands of God from whence this amazing gift of life came. God entrusts to them this child in the stewardship of parenthood; but that life forever belongs to God. T. S. Eliot captures this truth in *The Confidential Clerk:*

"Of course, there's something in us,
In all of us, which isn't just heredity,
But something unique. Something we have been
From eternity. Something . . . straight from God.
That means that we are nearer to God than to anyone."

The Pastor's Task in Family Crises

Families today are heir to so many threats and influences of
disintegration that the average pastor usually finds himself working with several family crises at the same time. A death in one
home, divorce in another, a long illness in still another: each of
these takes its toll of family solidarity, at the same time calling
forth from the pastor all that he has to give in counsel, comfort,
and aid.

Perhaps of all life's crises, our society is least able to accept
death. Morticians have disguised the facts of death with make-up
and artful caskets. Newspapers sometimes avoid the very word
and headline an obituary with " Alexander Doe Passes " as if
the fact were not quite to be believed. In our conversation we are
apt to use some awkward euphemism: " passed away," " gone
on," " no longer with us." Yet death is a part of life, and for it
the Christian should be ready all his days. Then when the end
comes both he and his family can accept with faith the inevitable
closing. The ministry to families in time of bereavement requires
more than a pastor; it requires a fellowship, and the church is
eminently prepared to bring the comfort that is needed.

In the day-by-day program of the church there is continuing
opportunity to help families prepare attitudes toward death. The
educational possibilities in the sermon, in Bible study and discussion, in church school are numerous. By these means the
reality of death can be discussed when there is no frightful emotional block in regard to the subject. Under such calm conditions
too, arrangements can be made for funerals so that when the
time does come the family will not overspend themselves in an
emotional frenzy. Prior funeral plans can be made with funeral
directors, with burial co-operatives, or with the church office.

There is no use pretending, though, that teaching people to

accept death in the abstract frees them from the shock that occurs when death comes home to them personally and tragically. The family may have profound faith in the goodness of God to provide a new home on the other side of death for their loved one; but their grief is tied to the here and now. In this common situation the church stands ready to do several helpful things: (1) the comfort of pastor and church friends means much at a time like this, and the planning of the funeral service can open up opportunities to recall to mind what elements of our faith concern life beyond death; (2) the pastor will be alert to minister to those who are suffering from heavy feelings of guilt and loss under these circumstances and to help them accept what cannot be changed; (3) the service itself, if handled in a concern for Christian verities and in good taste, will prove of inestimable comfort to the family; (4) invariably the Marthas of the congregation prepare food for the family so that they can forget this one detail and have no worry about meals, and this kindness is helpful far beyond the physical sustenance that it provides.

Entering the house of bereavement, the pastor is confronted with a host of basic, anguished questions. Here is to be found sorrow, guilt, shock, frustration, bewilderment, resentment, disillusionment, bitterness. Grief and guilt are so mingled in the feelings of the bereaved that the pastor must look sharply to tell the one from the other. In the family's anxiety around the death experience, they may repress whatever hostility they have been bearing; but they can hardly disavow their guilty feelings. How they treated the deceased, resentments they felt toward him, opportunities to be kind that they missed: these are the self-recriminations that come crowding in upon them. If he walked alone, the clergyman would now be pushed beyond his strength; but in God he has mighty assistance. He brings with him the comfort of a lively hope, his own faith in the promises of God through Christ, and the backing of a fellowship of the concerned. The faith to which he bears witness is expressed in his prayers, in his assurances of forgiveness, and in the memorial service that he leads. The fellowship of the concerned is expressed in their gifts of prayer, of food, of money, of assistance. Death, even as it pulls emotions apart, pulls people together. Ministering to a family in time of death can be the pastor's hardest job, but it can also be a privilege.

In the case of a child's death, the tragedy is heightened, and the pastor is put upon his mettle to bring any comfort at all into this loss. To be sure, he may occasionally find that the family is unusually brave, and that they minister to his sorrow; but in most cases he will find them shaken and grief-stricken. Here a firm Christian belief in immortality as a developing experience is essential, assuring that young lives in the hands of God will have at least as good a chance to develop into maturity on the other side of death as here. To interpret what God has provided beyond this life as static is neither comforting nor consistent with our theology. But parents wonder about more than the future of their child. They worry deeply over their own shortcomings as parents when their child was with them; they are laden down with guilt. The pastor does not in this instance act with easy reassurance that all will work out nicely, or that their guilt is unjustified. Instead he allows them to talk it out confidentially to him, permitting them to express emotions freely, trying to understand them and their sorrow. If under these circumstances he can lift to God a prayer that expresses the lostness and confusion of the family, appealing to Him who bears an eternal cross to touch this family with healing, the family may also find themselves at prayer, locating a renewed source of strength.

Christian fellowship through the priesthood of believers strengthens a family in their bereavement. Yet, as anyone can see, much of our preparation for sorrow must be made in times of joy. The church ought always to be preparing people for death, helping them to think through their faith so that when calamity strikes they will not be caught in a last-ditch attempt to form a living faith when they have so little to hang onto. If the church is engaged continually in its ministry of reconciliation, family relationships may be so strengthened that when tragedy strikes, the family will be somewhat ready, and their inevitable guilt might be better accepted. A touching article in *Parents'* magazine once told of how a mother had reconciled herself to losing a six-year-old son who had a terminal case of cancer. The family had pulled together their ranks and had faced the certainty of death by living each day to the full, spending the maximum time possible in experiences of joy, and fully relying upon their Christian faith (as any family should be doing) for day-to-day guidance. Something of that same high courage, something of that same thoughtful appreciation of the gifts of God, should underlie every family all the time; and the church that has a full ministry to Christian families will help them find these values.

When, however, it is an older person who dies, a different question emerges. How shall this be explained to the children? Often the question takes care of itself as youngsters, with more perception than they get credit for, sense the problem and end up comforting the adults. It is not particularly advisable for young children to be whisked out of the home when death has come as a rude, uninvited guest. They ought not to be shielded from the grief and sorrow their elders feel. It is better by far to let them remain. To hear the mysterious whispers of older people who shunt them out of the way increases their anxiety about some condition that they cannot understand. Later when they become aware of the death they may somehow blame themselves for this separation because it is associated in their minds with the mystery that surrounded it, and the way that they were removed.

If the funeral service, as you the pastor conduct it, is truly a worship service, emphasizing the Christian hope and playing down the extravagancies of emotionalism (and if it isn't, it ought to be), children can be present. The very sight and feel of a worship service in which God is thanked for his gift of life, with the great Scripture passages that pertain to death and life beyond, will strengthen the faith of a child. And he is helped by the community of wonder and of respect present in a truly Christian memorial service.

Many parents will need assistance in explaining the death of grandparent or brother to a child and will appeal to you for words and thoughts. To put into their hands the leaflet by Lewis K. Sherrill *Interpreting Death to Children* (five cents from the National Council of Churches) or to let them read the chapter on " Children and Death " from Dora Chaplin's *Children and Religion* will go a long way toward making clear to them what death is and what God has promised beyond it. But such bibliotherapy will not replace the minister's personal guidance wherein he needs to review with the adults themselves the great verities of the Christian promise about death and immortality. These doctrines are of comfort; but they are not dissociated from the message of the cross; and this must be frankly acknowledged. There is suffering to be borne; yet even our suffering can be offered up to God in Christ. For when they have straightened out their own confusion they are much better able to deal with that of their children. Indeed, their quest for the words to tell the story to children may be only a thinly veiled request for more assurance for themselves. The presence of death and our sublime faith in God's triumph over death can be explained by a parent, together with the pastor if desired, but with simple words and brief references to our firm reliance upon God. To answer the questions that the child will ask, and to teach him to lift his sorrow to God in prayer, will add notably to his growing faith.

In my own ministry I have found it especially comforting to return the very next Sunday evening to the home in which a death has occurred, and to lead the family in quiet worship. The intimate group gathered there at a time of mellowing grief needs a personal service of memorial and of comfort. Another time when a grieving family requires comfort is to be found in the succeeding holiday seasons when bittersweet memories crowd in upon them again. To leave some worship helps for them to use (Harry Emerson Fosdick's *The Assurance of Immortality* has not outlived its usefulness) enables them to continue family worship on their own with appropriate readings. These, of course, are not the final calls in the home, but in some ways they are most important. Calls that precede the funeral frequently come to people so numbed by shock that they are unaware of surroundings or of words. But now they have begun to realize more sharply and guiltily what has happened to them; and they are in real need of ministry. As time goes on, minister and church members will call and keep in touch with the bereaved household and this is as it should be. That ministry is most barren which drops a sorrowing family because the formalities have been taken care of.

Illness in the Family

Pastors are so accustomed to making sick calls and to dealing with the psychological ramifications of illness that it would be bootless here to treat the subject of pastoral care of ill persons. But it would not be amiss to remind that the pastor does have a secondary ministry to perform for the family of a sick or injured person. In fact, in those cases where the patient is in a coma, or beyond conscious communication, the family is clearly the pastor's primary concern. In any case it is well for him to remember that while the ill person is receiving attention and care, family members may feel so neglected as to harbor feelings of resentment against their ailing loved one.

Pastoral care of such a family may require nothing more profound than taking a little time with them, allowing for a long enough visit so that healthy members of the family will also have a chance to be ministered unto. They have worries about the sickness, the prognosis, the expenses, the new adjustments. Beneath these they have anxieties about questions that disturb deeply when they allow themselves to think about them. Ambivalent feelings that include both love and hate, barely concealed hostility toward a bed-ridden relative, guilt over impatience or irritation: these are common. Unless the pastor occasionally spends enough time with family members to let them talk out these worries and anxieties, they may smolder and cause unnecessary tension in the home.

In addition to the creative listening he does in such situations, the pastor has active ways of assisting families in times of illness. He is often the channel to organized succor from the congregation. The supplying of " sitters " to keep watch in the house while the family gets out for an hour, or the organization of house cleaners who relieve a weary mother of this chore so she can concentrate on nursing, the delivery of an occasional dessert for a treat: these come to the rescue when the pastor passes on the word. His role is truly a full one, and he is privileged to help in a number of ways. His is often the explanation that quiets fears and misunderstandings about what happens in a hospital. He is often there with the family, standing by in time of surgery. And daily as he lifts intercessions for his congregation, petitions for the healing of the sick head his prayer list.

For the chronically ill, most denominations have long published special materials in Christian education. The loose organization of those who are thus reached is sometimes called the Home Department, sometimes the Extension Department. In recent years, such outreach has been enlarged to include those who are temporarily compelled to miss church school — the acutely ill, mothers of infants, those who are employed on Sunday, people who live in remote areas, and even some who have rather too much inertia to get out of bed on Sunday morning. Home Department visitors assist the pastor in his calling as they deliver to such homes the church school curriculum materials for the confined person. This keeps them in touch with the fellowship, and offers an opportunity in independent study.

Mental illness is not altogether different in the effect it has upon a family, or in the kind of ministry necessitated by it. In his book *The Church and Mental Health,* Paul B. Maves tells of a pastor who helped a family get a young wife into a mental hospital where she was cured. When she was returned to her family, the pastor was present at the home-coming, and called occasionally thereafter to counsel with her and her family. She recovered, and her family was able to weather the storm. This pastoral care for the mentally ill is significant because it also took into account the family of the patient. Pastors nowadays call not only upon the person confined in a mental hospital but also on the family.

The mentally ill are often desperately lonely, feeling unaccepted and unacceptable. In truth, their families have sometimes made them feel unaccepted by frigid and confused attitudes. Other members of the family may withdraw from the psychotic family member because of their embarrassment or fear, a factor that only complicates their loved one's illness! The pastor can aid the family by interpreting the nature of mental illness, helping them to understand that it is a sickness that needs to involve no shame. With nearly a quarter million hospital beds filled by mental patients and an estimated nine million persons in the United States mentally upset but not hospitalized, this problem is too common to be regarded as mystery, and better understood than to be regarded now as a disgrace.

In the Netherlands, the standard method of treating mental illness is to acknowledge the family as a therapeutic group. Few patients are hospitalized, but are treated in their home environment among their family, their familiar surroundings, and their hobbies. Dr. A. Querido, professor of social medicine at the University of Amsterdam, finds "the most powerful means for [a patient's] future adjustment in the love he may feel for a child, in the self-sacrificing attitude of his wife, in his interest in tropical fish, or in his garden."

The idea of home treatment in mental illness is spreading into England, Israel, and the U.S.A. where Karl Menninger calls it "brains before bricks," i.e., the intelligent use of our resources rather than more and more hospital buildings. Much of the emphasis upon brains here refers to preventive medicine; and in the preventive side of mental health, there is no agency as powerful as a wholesome family. It is here the pastor can make a significant contribution in the education of his people.

Families Out of Reach

Families are also separated in these years of world tension by the demands of the draft. Pastors are growing accustomed to the duty of ministering to families of servicemen.

Men in the service still remain a part of their home church family when the pastor utilizes the connections that he has with their chaplains. He can introduce men to chaplains by a ministry of letter writing that will help his young men to feel more at home in chapel worship, and also aid the chaplain in his ministry to the men. A church that is alive to the possibility of ministering to servicemen and their families can see its ministry in four segments.

1. In the preparation of their youth for military service, the church will provide a relevant and effective program in the youth groups, counseling at graduation from high school, and special interviews at the time of induction.

2. When the man is in the service, he begins to receive mail from his church: personal letters from individuals and the pastor, Sunday bulletins for the servicemen themselves telling about the church and about the others who are in the service. If these letters that speak of the church's concern for their youth are mimeographed, there needs to be some appended note of a personal nature from the pastor or some member to make it more meaningful. Gifts at Christmastide, devotional booklets at regular periods, and Testaments are also sent.

Some churches have done still more. They have supplied lists of mission stations in the men's area, servicemen's lounges, and USO organizations of the area. Often the church office can send a return postal card for the men to write the church and keep the church posted about their address and the news about themselves.

3. At the same time, the pastor remembers that the family can use some ministry at this time of loneliness and worry. Calls to the home and the distribution of interpretive literature are of help, e.g., *Your Son,* published by the Presbyterian Committee on Chaplains and Service Personnel. Many denominations provide special materials for just this purpose. The result is that the serviceman does not lose touch with his parish at a time when he is at the age and condition that it is easy to drop the whole church idea, and that he is assured that the church still cares about him. Moreover, the families of servicemen are kept closer to the church; and the entire congregation remains conscious of its responsibility to this rapidly changing group. The Church can hardly bless the militarism and the armament race in which the nations are involved during these anxious years; but while

they deplore the national policies that make for such tragedy, they need also to minister to the many families caught in the system.

4. The fourth stage — a crucial one — comes when the service-man returns home. He is assured not only of a welcome but also of interviews with the pastor and referrals to employers, college, or further counseling such as the church can provide or locate.

Through the developmental stages of family life the pastor meets his people, and if he is sensitive to their need, he can minister to them effectually. In their times of joy when a child is born or when an illness is conquered, he goes to his people, sharing with them in rejoicing. In their times of crisis he is with them too, bringing comfort and support. At other times in their extremity they seek out the pastor to help them in their family problems. For such a time he requires some knowledge of the field of family counseling.

4

THE PASTOR
AS A FAMILY COUNSELOR

*All happy families resemble one
another; every unhappy family is
unhappy in its own fashion.* — Leo Tolstoy.

Hercule Poirot, as any follower of whodunit fiction knows, is a
little Belgian detective in the mystery novels of Agatha Christie.
In one of these, *The Peril at End House,* Hercule pronounced
what for him is an important principle: " The more prosaic explanation is nearly always the more probable " (pp. 109, 110).

Now, that observation might be of use in solving a murder
case, but it can hardly be transferred directly to family counseling. The deep and unseen wellsprings of human behavior are
apt to be neither prosaic nor very predictable at all. When, in addition, unpredictable behavior is complicated by those intimate,
interpersonal relationships which family life entails, the picture
becomes confusing indeed.

Family counseling has more dimensions than typical counseling about personal problems. Here the pastor's counseling task
is more intricate because he must be ever mindful of family relationships and how home life will be affected by this experience.
To work with a husband who is changing his attitudes and
making adjustments without also helping the wife to prepare
for such changes fails to fulfill the larger implications of family
counseling. To counsel with a teen-ager apart from understanding her involvements with parents accomplishes but half the
job. Family counseling is not just a consideration of problems in

the home (mixed marriages, juvenile rebelliousness, or family budget failure), but is more a concern with the relationships of people: a husband and wife, a teen-ager wresting emancipation from parents, a grandfather who is considered cantankerous.

Family counseling deals for the most part with normal people rather than with the psychoneurotic persons whose case histories are the stock in trade of counseling books and courses. They may be unusual folk in unusual jams; but they usually come under Dr. Lena Levine's definition of normalcy — only a slight neurosis. (See Lena Levine and Beka Doherty, *Women Needn't Worry*.) Their problems, in fact, tend to fall in clusters around life's predictable developmental stages. The adjustments required to a new baby, the feelings of emptiness when grown children leave home to begin their own families, the grief that follows the death of a loved one, the crises of gathering age: these are a few of the common developments in family life that bring counselees to the pastor's study. When they come for counseling they need to work through some of their feelings about relationships at home and elsewhere. For these developmental stages are the very stuff of conflict and of crises. Even if family counseling involves work with normal people who are confronted with problems common to us all, it necessitates careful pastoral work. When people are baffled enough about their problems to seek help, some anxieties will be present, and the pastor will need to custom-fit his interviews to the unique conditions of family counseling.

Family Counseling Is No Hobby

Counseling in family problems is no hobby, to be compared to wood turning, or matchbook collecting. When it is done conscientiously, such counseling is hard, enervating work whose moments of satisfaction are few and far between. Harry Stack Sullivan (*The Psychiatric Interview*) used to tell his medical students that anyone who thinks that psychiatric counseling is fun ought to steer clear of it entirely; he's not fitted for such labor. Similarly there are ministers here and there who have considered their pastoral counseling to be such a lark that they have made a specialty of it, often to the exclusion of other ministerial duties.

It can be said unqualifiedly that the minister who neglects his total calling in order to putter in counseling has not only neglected the basic function to which he has been called, but will doubtless do an indifferent job of counseling as well. For counseling of all sorts is now an integral part of a Christian pastor's work, fitting into his rounded vocation. In the long run, the personality of the pastoral counselor becomes as important as his techniques. If he is a spiritually mature person himself, who understands his own feelings and is usually able to manage them, if he studies and understands his theology, he will be more effective as a counselor. The clergyman is first, last, and always a theologian; and in that context is his counseling done. As one who understands Christian theology, he appreciates the infinite worth of a soul and does not despise the wretched persons who seek aid in their conflicts. He has enough faith in the gospel not to despair of hope; he is realistic about human weaknesses, recognizing sin and its depravity without forgetting the glorious possibilities that God has endowed in every man. Although not without some anxiety of his own, the pastor is able to accept his counselee even when that person is unacceptable to others. Indeed if God for Christ's sake is willing to forgive the most objectionable of sinners, it hardly belongs to the clergyman to reject parishioners whose works fail to justify them, for he too is still growing in his understanding of the gospel.

Again and again, the pastor will be hard put to make the doctrine of forgiveness meaningful to some disturbed soul who has wronged her husband or perhaps her child. To help such a one discover the infinite love and acceptance of God in Christ is a tremendous privilege. Not that God glosses over the transgression, but that God accepts one *in spite of* the transgression is the emphasis, for God's forgiveness and his judgment are ever fused. These separate sides of the same coin are expressed in his mercy and wisdom.

Far from seeming impossible, transformation of personality is viewed by the New Testament as realistic, something to be expected! " Do not be conformed to this world but be transformed by the renewal of your mind " (Rom. 12:2). " Therefore, if any one is in Christ, he is a new creation " (II Cor. 5:17). More profoundly centered than psychoanalysis, Christianity also has the faith that personality can be rebuilt for the better. As Carol Murphy points out in *The Ministry of Counseling* (p. 5):

" Christianity in its alivest periods did not conceive of the religious way as burdensome moralism but as joy and fulfillment, bringing the ability to be more than conqueror of any earthly circumstances. Those who read the writings of the greatest saints find there, even amid records of asceticism and suffering, the same note of newness of life and fresh perception of the beauty and omnipresence of the ultimate value, God."

Such a vision the pastor can communicate to those with family troubles when he is thoroughly steeped in his Bible and Reformation doctrines about the Christian family. It is indeed the pastor's roots in his faith and Christian knowledge that save him from trespassing into the psychotherapeutic fields where he ought not be caught. Karl Menninger, writing in *Pastoral Psychology,* spoke as a psychiatrist in criticizing much of the literature in this field as tending to " err a little on the side of encouraging the minister to undertake more therapy than I believe to be wise." Less politely restrained was the inside word from the late David E. Roberts in his *Psychotherapy and a Christian View of Man* that too many ministers seek to find psychological data on their parishioners when what they ought to be doing is clarifying their own doctrinal thinking! That clarification operation might save them from a great deal of grief, and contribute mightily toward the effectiveness of their counseling as well.

The hobbyist-counselor indeed has made his worst mistake in passing by his finest resource: Biblical theology. Prof. Wesner Fallaw agrees:

" Functionally, the pastor is a theologian, and this relatively new phase of the ministry, pastoral psychology, has found parsons striving diligently and wisely to make theology operationally effective. This is a correct and long overdue undertaking, for few there are who would deny that theology has tended to remain rigid to the point of demanding that persons serve it instead of its serving persons. It is right, I maintain, for pastoral psychology to attempt to bring the truths of Christian theology to the healing of emotionally troubled and spiritually sick people. It is precisely at this point that pastoral psychology and religious education meet, for both are to be denoted basically as a process of personal growth in Christian conduct. Both tap the resources of theology." (*Pastoral Psychology,* Oct. 1951, p. 19.)

In his day-to-day calling, the pastor has a tremendous amount of symbolic and real authority that is unmatched by any other profession. Often the physician or the psychiatrist would covet the passport that the minister has into the homes of his people. This privilege allows him to walk into a situation and rescue it from disaster where a stitch in time may save nine — or many more. Although this privilege must be used with discretion, and the exercise of it must be weighed always over against the consideration of whether more good can thus be gained than by waiting for them to take the initiative, it can be of inestimable value. The clergyman's opportunities are amazing because his field is life itself, and his function to bring others into the presence of Him who came that they might also have life — abundantly.

"Gnothi Sauton"

Socrates had a brief admonition that the world has never forgotten: Gnothi sauton — Know thyself! It is a word of peculiar importance to the minister-counselor. Unless he is aware of himself, his strengths and weaknesses, and has some understanding of his own feelings, he will fail in counseling. It is imperative, moreover, that he be a self-accepting, adjusted individual, for he who cannot accept himself is unable to accept others. In seeking to be noncoercive the counselor does not lack opinions. He has a point of view but is honest enough to know that his ideas are those of just one person, to be respected and revised just as others' viewpoints are. If he understands his own prejudices and yet is able to remain free from them as he counsels, he can respect the parishioner's point of view.

He will also be able in time to accept the counselee as a person and to abide whatever objectionable characteristics he has. Few have so cogently stated the case for self-acceptance as has William Graham Cole in his book *Sex in Christianity and Psychoanalysis* (pp. 307–308):

"Self-acceptance, which is absolutely indispensable to loving others ('Love thy neighbor as thyself'), is possible only through being accepted. This is the significance both of the gospel which announces that God loves men while they are yet sinners and of the psychoanalytic acceptance of the patient. The neurotic on the couch has grown up believing that no one can love him as he is, that he must constantly conform to the wishes and expectations of others if he is to win their approval, and he bitterly resents the demands made on him. He tries desperately to impress and to win the analyst, discovering only gradually and painfully that such tactics are both futile and unnecessary. This was the problem of the Pharisees, at least as they are portrayed in the New Testament, whatever may have been true of them historically; they thought they had to earn the divine love and acceptance by being good. Rejecting themselves as they actually were, they set up an ideal image of themselves as they believed they ought to be and then attempted to prove to themselves and to everyone else that they were actually conforming to that ideal image. The apostle Paul experienced the failure of such an effort and learned, as the analysand must learn, that acceptance and love are gifts, not payments for services rendered."

The pastor's ability to live with himself is essential to his preparation to counsel with others about their own conflicts. He should never be so unwise as to come to his counseling task without adequate preparation in prayer. Through his daily devotional life, he must recall on his prayer list those who, in the words of *The Book of Common Prayer,* "are any ways afflicted, or distressed in mind, body, or estate " (" A Prayer for All Conditions of Men," p. 19). If in his habitual worship, his practicing of the presence of God, he seeks spiritual strength to supplement his own, and God's wisdom to increase his, he will not feel that he stands alone when he is confronted by some of life's most frustrating problems.

Nor need the pastor feel alone when he is part of a church fellowship. There is here a safeguard in that while the individual minister may not be altogether sagacious in his counseling relationship, he is representative of a fellowship which at its Christian best is therapeutic. Dr. Otis Rice, chaplain of St. Luke's Hospital in New York City, once said in an address:

"The Church itself is founded as a fellowship symbolic of the family. With all its mistakes and defects it has held the family in the center of its thinking and ministry and has in the past done much to create those healthy family groups out of which come mature and rich-minded individuals. It is my own belief that the Church can assimilate new insights and understandings with respect to the family and can continue to be a vital force in educating its members for healthy family life and in preserving the richness and creativity of the unit essential to both society and the Church — the family."

That First Interview

The first counseling interview may be the only one there ever is. It may be the only help that a parishioner gets in a given case of family crisis. Books on professional counseling too often take for granted a severely structured counseling situation with office hours, secretary, and continuing contacts. The sober fact is that much of the minister's counseling must be catch-as-catch-can in the church study, along the street while waiting for the traffic light to change, in homes, and restaurants. Sometimes strangers drop into the church office and do not return; frequently church folk who wish to appear casual about their needs visit just once and will not return for a long time again.

But sometimes, let it be frankly admitted, the reason that our counselees do not return to us is that we botch the job in the first interview. Perhaps we let them tell too much of their intimate difficulties and allow them to create more anxiety than they can handle. They then feel that they dare not face us again. It may be that we fail to perceive a deeper problem beneath that which is presented, and someone goes away disappointed because neither he nor his counselor was able to speak of the basic fear that he feels. It may be that we did not listen for the indication of deep-lying feeling that we might have heard, had we only possessed more insight.

To get on rapport with the counselee in his very first visit re-

quires not only the natural endowment of friendliness and understanding but also experience in handling these initial contacts.
The atmosphere of this encounter is important: the very avail-
ability of the counselor, the unhurried spirit of receptivity, the
cheerfulness that is not too hearty, the interest that is not intru-
sive. Much of this atmosphere has been set up in advance by the
kind of remarks that a pastor makes, by the degree of kindliness
people discover in him, the sort of opinion they hear in his sermons, and the way he makes his calls in the parish.

There is no gainsaying that techniques make a real difference.
Techniques can be learned and their use can be improved with
practice. To be able to listen responsively and creatively, to maintain a listening interview that yet is not directionless, to convey
understanding without rushing the insights of the counselee:
these require a knowledge of techniques and their use.

The experienced counselor does not promise glowing results
for the family crisis. He formulates with the counselee the family problem and describes it carefully in order to evaluate it and
judge whether the solution of the problem would actually be
acceptable to the family if it means some sacrifice. He is satisfied
with limited goals that may change the balance in the problem
and make the family's life more stable. It is perfectly defensible
to subscribe to Otto Rank's view that not every maladjustment
can be unwound back to its beginnings and reconstructed. (See
Will Therapy; and, Truth and Reality.) Sometimes it is enough
to relieve the current tensions and to make the situation more
tolerable.

Realism requires that the counselor then pull together in summary some of the possible steps that can be taken, citing the resources at hand in family strength, community facilities, religious help, and personal assets of the client's position. The
problem must be clarified, gathering only those data which are
relevant and provide for the parishioner to marshal his strength.
In all this, the counselor shows his warmth and interest. Whatever solution is reached has to be described within the limits of
the case: the counselee's own personal characteristics and not
those he might wish for that are beyond his present grasp, the

counselee's family group and not some imaginary wife he phantasies or some other home he might desire instead.

Few family problems are isolated from the general character of the whole person. Marriage difficulties, for instance, are not unrelated to a person's adjustment pattern in all his contacts. A family problem that involves years of bitterness will not be solved in one hour of sharing; but to help a troubled person get out his feelings about himself and his contacts is a start to discovering how he sees himself in his home. Breakdowns in family life are much like breakdowns in other human relationships.

Anyone who summons up the courage to seek you out for help has already mulled over a number of possible solutions to his problem, but has been unable to discover how to use any one of them. The counselor's task is to get him to describe what he has already considered, and to help him weigh these possibilties to make his own choice. The counselor listens with enough empathy to understand feelings, and enough detachment to keep the counselee responsible for his own decision.

The average parishioner who finally brings himself to the courageous step of seeking help is full of doubts and defense mechanisms; the counselor who realizes this will get farther faster. Common defense mechanisms include denial, rationalization, and projection. But it is not the pastor's cue to knock these props completely out; the troubled person has to be allowed to retain some of his defenses. None of us can avoid denying guilty feelings, or rationalizing our course of action as the only right or defensible one, or projecting our own situation onto someone else in blame or in criticism. Readers may recall how Amanda Wingfield was forever projecting her own desire for popularity upon her unattractive daughter, Laura, supplying the emotional content of Tennessee Williams' play *The Glass Menagerie*. To understand these defense mechanisms is to understand something of the dynamics that make counseling possible — and difficult. Our people come to us only after overcoming their inertia and giving up the hope to keep their crisis a secret. Some also must overcome a fear of being obligated to the pastor; they must also cope with their sense of shame and guilt.

Not to recognize the considerable content of guilt in such contacts is to miss a chance to be helpful. Ministers are too prone to
intellectualize and to forget that the human organism lives
more on the feeling level than on the cognitive. Just because the
pastor can think through the problem and see a solution does
not insure that the parishioner will accept that solution and act
upon it. Real counseling consists of helping people to find resources *within themselves* to work out their own solutions, a
process that does not mean jolting the person. The object of
counseling is not to pull the crutch out from under a man, but to
help him stand straight so that a crutch is no longer needed.

Throughout formal counseling (and the pastor is increasingly
involved in this kind), every interview is different from every
other, and there is no jig by which they may be cut for mass
production. Counseling, contrary to the simple popular notion,
is not to be compared to a fortunetelling machine in the penny
arcade where one points to the area of his question, inserts his
coin, and then watches the answer light up. In counseling, we
never reach the end of the assembly line and we never have perfectly fitting interchangeable parts. There are no all-pervading
specific directions in counseling because this is a living process
confronted by real persons who have a God-given refractory nature that rebels against sudden decisions and clerical maneuver-
ing.

What then passes between a pastor who has a deep concern
for his people and a person troubled by some family difficulty is
a dynamic relationship well named by Harry Stack Sullivan in
The Psychiatric Interview as a " two-group." Essentially in his
counseling the pastor sees the importance of the interview as a
process of accepting the person where he is, and going from
there, of asking questions that root out the *attitude* of the person
toward his situation, and of accepting these attitudes without
moralizing. These he discusses calmly with him, recognizing
sympathetically that guilt and anxiety are altogether natural feelings that do not fall under the pastor's stern judgment. The pastor who is able to understand these things and act upon them in
counseling will realize that when a person talks out his difficul-

ties and the way he feels, he is going to reap more satisfaction than he would from any amount of prescribed information or advice.

Beware of These Booby Traps

Family counseling experiences are cluttered by a series of booby traps, a few of which are set by the scheming machinations of neurotic parishioners, but most of which are unwittingly placed there by the unwary counselor himself when he is not self-accepting or when he has not learned yet to discipline his work and use his abilities wisely. Some of the most common of these are:

1. *The do-sit-down-and-let-me-help-you spirit.* Astonishing as it sounds at first, there is a fallacy in mere helpfulness. At first blush it would appear that one who wants to be helpful must be a person of real magnanimity and generosity; but our unconscious desires growing out of our self-image and former relationships can so skillfully camouflage real motivations that even this seeming altruism is often loaded as a trap. Like the domineering church officer who wangles committee work in order to get management into his own hands, our ego-centered impulses sometimes cloak the will-to-power under an appearance of self-sacrifice.

The late Fritz Künkel in his stimulating study *What Do You Advise?* (p. 186) calls this spade just that when he writes:

"No one should want to 'help' other people. The more we want to help them the less we are able to help them. That is why relatives and married people can seldom help each other; nor can people in love cure each other of their neuroses. In order to understand this, let us trace the source of this desire to help, which is the rock on which so many good counseling ships (and other relationships) founder.

"If we wish to help other people, it is because we have already judged them to be in the wrong. We evaluate another human being. We set ourselves in the place of God; or at least we think of ourselves as saints, or perhaps as redeemers, whose task it is to reconcile our fellows with God. Our capacity to help others is caged within

this tight little prison of self-esteem. We graciously extend a strong
hand to our sinking neighbor. But from the client's point of view,
we are dupes. [A client] . . . would see beneath our self-esteem to
the human vanity and weakness below. Next time she wished to gain
the advantage, she would repeat the performance which forced us to
show pity, gladness, or annoyance — all evidences of the power she
has over us. She is a better strategist, and a more powerful one, than
we; and she will win every time. But the counselor knows that her
'winning' is actually a loss: she loses her inner battle against developing egocentricity, in order to 'win' her outer battle against other
people.

"The counselor who wishes to help contributes to [her] . . .
greater loss by falling into the trap of his own egocentric vanity.
Learning this again and again, as every counselor must, he realizes
that after all he too is only human. It is just as important that the
helper's egocentricity be resolved as that [the client] . . . resolve
hers. The objective goal of counseling is never to help another individual to be more like the counselor's preconceived ideal. Our aid
must always be to study the maturing personality; to observe the way
that it functions; and through our own impartial interest, to give
the client courage to study himself."

The last thing that the counseling minister ought to expect is
gratitude from his counselees. But the workings of our pride are
so insidious that somewhere lies the expectation that after we
have been " helpful " in some family problem, the counselee will
be thankful. That way lies disillusion, well deserved.

The overly " helpful " counselor may also foster an unhealthy
dependency relationship with clients and find himself with a
problem he would like to shake off but cannot. Under such circumstances he may compound the felony by becoming brusque
and harsh in an effort to get out from under the attachment.
Had he taken a more realistic view of his counseling role to begin
with, this might not have developed. A counselor less ego-
centered will focus upon aiding the parishioner to find a solution
instead of playing the part of the Great Big Helper. The experienced counselor even knows the value of what Ernest R.
Groves in *Christianity and the Family* used to call " a sacrifice
hit in counseling," where he cares nothing for credit and is will-

ing even to receive the hostile regard of the client in order to work through the problem.

Some such problems may be alleviated if the pastor himself has had a counselor. Every pastor needs a pastor; for his work is a lonely work, and to keep balanced, he requires a confidential relationship with someone (not his wife!) who can help him share his concerns. His wife has too many relationships to maintain in the parish to be burdened by confidential information about those people; but many ministers have formed a team with some physicians and psychologists in which they can work together on problems of mutual interest. Such a team accomplishes more than any one of them working alone, and together they share the load.

In time the practicing counselor learns to be cautious about his promises to help. More realistically he speaks in such terms as: "I can't tell you what to do; but I'll work with you on this problem. Together we'll try to find a solution."

2. *The now-just-tell-me-your-problem approach.* If ever there is an approach that gives away a counselor's inner craving to satisfy his curiosity, this one is it. Eager to collect some data on the parishioner and his family, and not at all averse to hearing some interesting scandal, the counselor's ears can almost be seen flapping. It's a risky business to encourage a counselee to open intimate doors to family closets and their skeletons. Yet the fascinating nature of such material may unwisely prompt the would-be counselor to invite it.

The booby trap ought to be obvious here; but such is our ability to fool ourselves that we may fail to see it. This is one good way to make a parishioner hate you — better by far even than dismissing an inept church school teacher. The counselee who tells too much about guilt-laden material can but feel sharp anxiety after leaving and he cannot be blamed for wanting never to see his pastor again.

Rev. Eutychus Zwingli (in reporting case histories I go to any unreasonable lengths to disguise names) became known widely in his West Coast city for being able to patch marital rifts. Couples with tensions consulted him, and he probed their lives thoroughly as an aid to reconciliation. He was successful both in bringing sparring partners into harmony and also in prying out unsavory details about their marital history. After a time he was astounded to receive a discreet visit from an informal church committee who requested that he take his time, but that he find a new pastorate in another locale. On that committee were two persons whom he had counseled during marriage crises. Whatever the full reason for their decision, this played a part: he knew too much about them now for them to be comfortable about having him as their minister any longer.

The pastor's work is different from that of the psychiatrist in a number of ways. The psychiatrist can deal with the personal material of his patients, keep a professional contact with them in appointments, and in the end dismiss them without further contacts. The pastor, on the other hand, has to live with his church members, see them weekly, and keep as cordial a relationship with them as with an employer. It's a striking difference.

Although the pastor must serve as a confessor to his repentant people at times, the purpose is to assist them to find forgiveness and a new way of handling their most troublesome relationships. When the emphasis is kept upon this positive goal, mishaps are less apt to occur.

The pastor, experienced in counseling, learns how to ration his questions and how to ask them. Questions should be few in number and not exhaustive, used to guide the interview rather than to probe for facts. When the interview stalls, a well-placed question might be asked, or the pastor may choose to review the goals with which they began: "Let's see, when we began, our hope was to find some way for you and your son-in-law to get along better. How far have we come in that?" But if the interview is scattered with long silences, it will not be harmful. These are times of thought that can be times of reconstruction. If they grow overly long and the counselor needs to recall his client to the project at hand, he might repeat the last thing that the client has said and let him add to that. In no case should he interrupt with a new direction lest he intercept an insight that is struggling to be born.

The reticent parishioner who finds it difficult to talk in the counseling setting may be encouraged to jot down notes between appointments and bring them with him. Much happens as an afterthought to counseling and is advanced through subsequent mulling. If then the parishioner writes down in letter form ideas to bring along, the next interview may be more productive than the last. The pastor must place responsibility for progress exactly where it belongs — on the person who has the family problem and who must make whatever movement is to be made. To get a parishioner to discover how much he is willing to sacrifice in order to work through his difficulty is to find a fair gauge to his seriousness in seeking counsel.

Soon or late the pastor discovers that it is not possible to reach an ultimately perfect solution to every quandary, but that to reduce a problem to its most manageable proportions may be all he can do. And that in the long run is a great deal.

3. *The just-take-my-advice approach.* The superior attitude of the voluntary adviser is hard to abide, often objectionable to the advised. Any Rev. Mr. Fixit who offers advice to his people bids fair to deserve what comes of it. He may thereafter find himself saddled by a dependency relationship that he cannot buck off, a weak individual who calls upon him often for every little decision. Worse yet, he may find himself blamed for some marriage failure because the couple took his advice seriously only to find that for them it did not work!

Annette Garrett, whose useful little book *Interviewing, Its Principles and Methods* has been a valuable reference for social workers, has this cogent observation about dispensing advice: " It is a temptation to work out a solution in full detail, especially when working with children or old people, but this temptation must be resolutely resisted. It is better to have a few details wrong but to have the client feel that the plan is one he has been instrumental in developing and is carrying out, with help to be sure, but essentially on his own initiative " (p. 122).

What a foolish denial of the counseling principle it is to prevent the counselee from learning to stand upon his own feet! The pastor who trips this booby trap soon rues his action, and wants to let go of the problem he has created but finds it too thorny either to handle or to release. The best that can be hoped is that the experience will be instructive so that the next time he is tempted to offer a prescription this error will be avoided.

It may even protect him from that inexcusable transgression occasionally committed by naïve pastors who step out of their profession and offer legal or even medical advice. In that direction can be found the occasional lawsuit for malpractice.

The insouciance of the professional adviser is difficult to take. We must realize that we cannot alter other people to be like ourselves. Respect for our counselee allows us to recognize that he is different from us, and we can recognize our differences as valid even though we cannot agree. Such an attitude on our own part permits us to maintain our integrity and the right to our own opinions even though we do not foist them upon our counselee. The prognosis is much more helpful when the counselee knows where we stand and participates actively in the process.

4. *The see-here-you-poor-soul pose.* Incredible as it seems in this age of enlightenment when nearly every newspaper and magazine poses as a kindly family counselor, some clergymen still are judgmental in their counseling. When the leery parishioner hesitantly comes to the study, half expecting his minister to be moralistic and judgmental, he finds his worst fears realized. Unable to confine his preachments to the pulpit, Rev. John Savonarola continues his homiletics in the counseling role. All too willing to place blame or to foment guilt on the part of the counselee, this chap does more harm than good. Confused about his function, he is apt to excuse himself by averring that it is his place to uphold Christian morality and to make that position abundantly clear. Yet the parishioner who comes to his pastor already knows any clergyman's position on adultery, polygamy, or child-beating. The parishioner needs help, not pulpiteering.

Being imperfect himself, and knowing as he looks upon the man who is in trouble that " there but for the grace of God go I," the Christian pastor will not condemn the person who strays from the path of righteousness and prudence. Rather he will seek to help him to find healing and new strength. The moral deviation after all is but a symptom of some deeper disturbance. As William Graham Cole describes the counselor in his *Sex in Christianity and Psychoanalysis* (p. 323):

"He will not become perfect; his trust will falter and his faith will fail. He will lust in his heart, but he will not despair. He will rather seek to keep his mind and heart filled with the knowledge and love of God and will run with patience the race that is set before him, looking unto Jesus, the author and finisher of his faith."

Judgment of the client throws up a block and impedes the real counseling movement toward the feelings of the client. And it is on those feelings that the counselor must focus. Beginners in counseling tend to waste time concentrating upon the problem presented to them; in time they learn to get into the deeper need that provokes that problem. Our behavior is rooted in emotion, not in intellect; and no counselor is successful in treating the emotions with logic.

It sometimes happens that the client's emotional stress is expressed in the interview through an eruption of tears. If that happens, or if other discomfort or pain is loosened, it should not baffle the pastor. The tactic is to wait it out — do not attempt to soothe the strain or shorten the period. Reach into the desk drawer for that ever-ready box of handkerchief tissues and pass them over. Stay with the client patiently as he struggles to speak about the things that affect him deeply.

5. *The cheer-up-and-forget-it heartiness.* Excessive heartiness is often the mark of a man who is impatient to get on with it. In a hurry to rush on to other things, such a parson pats the distraught person on the back and attempts to laugh off the feelings of insecurity that counselee (and counselor) feel at the time. The pastor with the ever-hurried, ever-busy schedule may actually have overcrowded it because at heart he is not a warm, kindly person; and he needs somehow to cover up his coldness with an appearance of haste and heartiness. He may also fear his own negative feelings, and play the role of a hearty person to cover them.

A widowed mother of our acquaintance traveled to a college

town where her daughter was to enter as a freshman, and there they met two pastors of the community. Hoping that in one of them the daughter would find a spiritual adviser to serve as a parent-surrogate, she met with and chatted with each. Afterward she asked her daughter to which of these men she would go if she needed to talk over a problem. The girl unhesitatingly named the plainer, less impressive of the two, the minister of a small mission church. " Why," asked the interested mother, " do you choose him? " Promptly the girl replied, " Because he is kind."

Kindness, however, is not a pose that can be ordered at will; it is built into character. Still, all of us are more capable of consideration when we are not too fatigued, not too rushed, and when we have disciplined ourselves through worship and re-creation to wait upon the Lord, and renew our strength in order to run and not be weary, to walk and not faint.

The hearty, backslapping parson tends to give too much reassurance to his clients. Reassurance has a nasty way of acting as a boomerang in counseling — it can make the disturbed person even more anxious when he concludes (what else could he conclude?) that this easy assurance is an indication that you fail to understand him. Harry Stack Sullivan, ever perceptive about these booby traps of counseling, writes into his *The Psychiatric Interview* (p. 227) : " You cannot do magic with reassuring language. The magic occurs in the interpersonal relations, and the real magic is done by the patient, not by the therapist. The therapist's skill and art lie in keeping things simple enough so that something can happen; in other words, he clears the field for favorable change, and then tries to avoid getting in the way of its development."

Instead of conning a counselee with unearned reassurance, let the pastor listen appreciatively, giving complete attention to the person. The disciplined counselor listens creatively, taking an occasional note (if this does not disturb his counselee) to keep a summary or to indicate a point of return. Simple records of the interview, carefully coded to prevent identification by chance discovery or prying eyes, are essential to the movement of counseling and to the counselor's ability to learn from his work.

Aware of the part that repression (the unconscious tendency to exclude painful or unpleasant ideas from one's thought), negative feelings, and/or the fear of hostility play in counseling, the disciplined counselor takes his work too seriously to assure his people to cheer up and forget it all. The pastor so often plays the role of "the professional good man," to borrow a repulsive description which Sinclair Lewis gave to Elmer Gantry, that he must be alert to separate his own feelings and his conditioning from the desire to be reassuring. Neither ill-timed jokes nor excessive heartiness have any place in the true empathy and supportive relations that much of our counseling requires.

If it is a busy schedule and haste that provokes the pastor into the cheer-up-and-forget-it heartiness, he can learn to utilize other resources to share the counseling load. Like Rev. Roy Burkhart of the First Community Church in Columbus, Ohio, he can train laymen to take certain counseling tasks of supportive nature and organize nurture groups for mutual therapy. Mothers clubs, councils of parents with retarded children, or classes for engaged couples are organized around these developmental tasks for just such a purpose. Or it is possible to suggest appropriate reading to the counselee to stimulate his self-help between interviews. Bibliotherapy, as this procedure is sometimes dubbed, has its limitations; and it should not include technical or lengthy books. Yet the kind of pamphlet made available through the Public Affairs Committee (e.g., *Saving Your Marriage, So You Think It's Love, Planning a Family,* etc.) admirably fills the bill. In our own experience through the Pastors' Seminars in Family Counseling, we developed a series of brief leaflets written about rather standard family problems under the general title "The Christian Family Faces Crisis." Published at five cents each by the Board of Christian Education of the Presbyterian Church in the U.S.A., they have covered such subjects as: *When Alcoholism Invades the Family; Conflicts in the Home; Facing Disappointment in the Family; The Family on a Shrinking Budget; The Employed Mother; When Daddy Is Drafted; Missing! — One Parent; Older Persons in the Home; The Handicapped Child in Your Home.*

Timing may be the pastor's main difficulty when he is too hearty. Not knowing how to organize his time, he attempts to laugh off the person's problem. *O tempora, O mores!* This is inexcusable. Instead, he can control the time through such stratagems as (1) saying to the parishioner on a crowded day: " We can spend twenty-five minutes together, so take your time and tell me about it. If we should not finish, we can meet again next Thursday "; or (2) setting up a series of hourly interviews for several weeks so that the parishioner sees these as a serious business with limitations that call forth his or her own participation; and then (3) spacing out these interviews to biweekly and then monthly or longer intervals in order to set the parishioner free on his own strength when that time has been reached. Such are some alternatives to ill-placed heartiness in the counseling relationship.

C. S. Lewis has pungently said that no one can go on forever being " a good egg." Sooner or later he will either have to turn bad — or hatch! The counselor can never use the " good egg " pose. People don't " cheer up and forget " deep anxieties. A more disciplined, prayerful ministry is required.

6. *The I-know-just-how-you-feel angle.* Watch this one. It implies rather more empathy than the pastor really ought to feel. It has all the earmarks of taking sides with the counselee in his interpersonal conflicts. To become too sympathetic with one adversary in a marital or family battle not only is dangerous to parish harmony but also is likely to throw sand in the eyes of the counselor so that he can no longer objectively see the problems of the people involved.

In the Marriage Council of Philadelphia it is a truism of the staff that the first person to reach the counselor's ear in some marital dispute could so present the case as to win sympathy and approval, but it pays to withhold conclusions about culpability until both viewpoints are seen. Often the counselor tends to identify with one partner against the other unless he is aware of his own feelings. To take sides obviously disqualifies him from effective counseling.

Too sympathetic an attitude toward the wife can cause gossip. Too close an identification with the cause of the husband may amount to false assurance, and result in something less than counseling — a simple reassuring word to cover up the pastor's insecurity about working with the problem.

Instead of feigning understanding when it is really absent, the counselor needs to acknowledge his lack of understanding and state it frankly. " I don't quite understand that " is a remark that often brings clarification not only for the counselor but even to the client as he attempts to recast his statements. But it may be that no amount of explanation will bring a clear understanding between a counselor and client of different races or backgrounds. And it may be, as Ernest Groves used to teach, that wanting to understand can be as important to the client as complete understanding (*Conserving Marriage and the Family*). In any case, the experienced counselor learns that an attempt to understand the person does not mean that he must condone all his acts and feelings. To accept the person does not necessitate accepting his actions.

The pastor who himself has known suffering and failure is already given some qualification to share the deep feelings of his people. To be sure, suffering may embitter as often as it mellows; and yet the Christian minister who has surmounted his own experiences of tragedy and trauma will develop an empathy that others will not acquire for years. Nevertheless he is not justified in using his personal experience as a recollection in counseling because it almost usurps the person's right to his own troubles. This is, after all, the counselee's problem, not the counselor's; and an attitude of sympathetic detachment may be the best position in average cases. The pastor as counselor must also think of the other family members and remain sufficiently objective (even though aware that there is no such thing as true objectivity) to bear in mind the welfare of the home from which his parishioners come.

Then knowing that he too has feelings, the counselor will less likely get caught in a dangerous situation of transference he cannot handle (transference being that condition in which the parishioner unconsciously assigns to the counselor a personal role in keeping with his past or present emotions — considering him as a father, a lover, or a hated authority). Transference is one of those warnings that referral is needed to psychological help. Likewise he will keep aware of the client's ambivalence (feeling contrary emotions of love and hate or dependence and independence at the same time). The pastoral counselor may never know just how a counselee feels, but in time he learns how others use their feelings, and are used by them. This is as close as he needs to come.

7. *The let-us-pray pose*. Surely a pastor's approach to his work ought to be prayerful, and it seems sacrilegious to suggest that some pastoral counselors might hide behind prayer rather than do the hard work that honest counseling requires. But such, alas, is the case. To avoid facing hard facts, or hostile reactions, the pastor may just take recourse in folded hands and closed eyes.

Many a nondirective interview has been closed with a very directive prayer! Those of us who sit on the pew side of the pulpit have sometimes noticed how the preachers are able to use the closing prayer to slip in an additional point to the sermon, or to emphasize the text in a brief summary. The same mistaken technique is used in counseling by the man who expresses aloud in prayer to God the things he did not feel comfortable about expressing to his counselee. There's a nasty name for this kind of practice. The New Testament calls it hypocrisy. Coercion by piety is as unprincipled as it is futile.

True, it may be better to err on the side of praying overmuch rather than not enough. And perhaps we more often make the mistake of omitting prayer than including it. Wayne Oates is right in his contention that the whole interview should be a prayer. But the earnest prayer of the pastor offered " in his closet " through private devotions or in silence can be just as sincere and far less anxiety-producing to some neurotic counselee. If a parishioner requests prayers, the way is clear (and in our pastoral calling, we frequently find that prayer is advisable also when not requested), but even then it is well for the pastor to separate carefully exaggerated piety from sincerity. Religiosity is frequently used to avoid real responsibility; and the Christian pastor more than anyone else is ready to defend true religion. The pastor ought never to seem to put off upon God the solution for a problem that needs hard thinking and real work. Neither should he ever come into a work as challenging as counseling except from his knees. With God we will discuss our counseling task rather than in gossip with friends.

In counseling, let it be reiterated, we are dealing with feelings, and feelings are changed only in a significant relationship with someone or with Someone. We can aid the counselee to explore his feelings. We can motivate a change; but it is up to him to make it. As pastors we always hold out hope for a solution not because of our human abilities but because of God. This is the ultimate relationship wherein the most profound changes occur.

5

PREPARATION AND GUIDANCE
FOR MARRIAGE

*If technical sex education were
all there is to premarital
guidance, a couple could be trained
for marriage in less than fifteen minutes.*

— Ernest R. Groves.

In "The Retroactive Existence of Mr. Juggins," Stephen Leacock parodied once and for all the elaborate preparations that
sometimes precede marriage. Mr. Juggins had fallen in love and
really intended to marry the girl, but he wasn't the kind to rush
into marriage without first preparing for that important step. So
he went into moral training by teaching a Sunday school class.
Soon, however, he realized that in order to be an effective teacher
he needed to undertake a serious study of the history of Palestine.
But then he felt he would be a cad to force his intentions on a girl
while only partially acquainted with Israelitish history, so he
stayed away from her for two years until he felt truly fit to pro-
pose. Of course by the time he had pronounced himself ready,
she was married to a man who didn't know Moses from Ahab.

Now pastoral care for the homes of tomorrow is not meant to
involve such intricate preparations and delays that the desired
outcome is defeated. Still, if the truth were known, the clergyman's concern for the marriages of the future and the families
of the new generation does not begin early enough. Premarital
guidance is most effective when it begins in the early years of
childhood while attitudes are being formed and the first impressions about family life are observed. Here the child gets his

earliest sex education — in attitudes, mark you — as he witnesses the love (or its lack) between his parents. Moreover, his own adjustment to family living begins to develop whatever degree of skill he will later acquire in those interpersonal relationships that make or break family life.

All this we know and quickly review as the truisms of child development within the family. What we seem to admit less readily is the potential influence of the pastor upon the children of his parish as they grow toward the day when they marry and begin new homes. Yet this influence also begins very early; and it too comes about by means of relationships. Fortunate is the minister who in his dealings with children is relaxed and accepting enough to answer their questions, deal with their doubts, and counsel them in their special problems. His contacts with children occur in calls to their homes, on visits to their church school departments, or through chance encounters on the street. If he is sensitive to their needs and conscious of children as individuals, the pastor will find himself counseling with boys and girls of the parish while they are still quite young. The minister who knows that children have worries (there is a canard in that phrase "carefree children") will work at teaching them that church is a friendly place. Frequent visits to children's classes for his story-telling or occasional substituting for a teacher will stand him in good stead with the small fry. He can enter into their recreational and fellowship activities so that they come to know him as a warm human person and grow to trust him as a friend.

Early in their school career the pastor can schedule once-a-year interviews with children of the church constituency. Usually such talks are light and friendly, but some involve real problems. In either case, these talks lead to an easy acceptance of the counseling relationship, and as the children grow older they become accustomed to dropping in and discussing frankly with him the things they feel are important. Moreover, the church educational program, for which the pastor ultimately is responsible, can gear into training for family life. Many curriculum lessons now deal with questions of family relationships, helping church school pupils of all ages to understand better their life with parents or with siblings, and something of their responsibility for the homes of tomorrow. By later childhood and early youth, youngsters in our churches are ready for education in a Christian interpretation of sex. They ought to know, as Dr. Nadina Kavinoky says, that "reproduction is the most normal event in life. The human body has been developing its capacity to reproduce for millions of years. No chemical or physical process is so complex or remarkable as that involved in reproduction. The intricate interplay of psychological, glandular, nutritional, and muscular factors is a masterful achievement of nature. Young people need to know the facts associated with childbirth so that this knowledge will dissipate the vague fears or tensions they must have." (*Education for Marriage,* by James A. Peterson, p. 279.) All this they need to know, but more must be added; our young people ought also to see a clear connection between this wonderful event of reproduction and the God who created us.

When they become young people, they need still more help than information on reproduction. They require today a code to help them handle their own sex drives. The subject of sex is so loaded with emotion that any comprehensive educational approach has some hazard. Sex information could be stimulating enough to cause the imaginative or erotic person to wish to experiment. Yet Lester Kirkendall in his definitive study *Sex Education as Human Relations* questioned 180 boys (who are more quickly aroused by sex information than girls) as to whether this education had increased or decreased their desire. Only eleven replied that they had felt such education had increased sexual desire. And, whether the education had come from parents, school, or church, these cases of increased desire had nearly always been linked with evasive answers.

To explain the nature of sex as if it is a remote subject to be appreciated in distant years is totally unrealistic for today's young people. A teen-age girl needs also to know what to do about demands for petting. She needs an understanding of the difference between the arousal threshold in boys and girls. She may be satisfied by affectionate words and caresses, but a boy's drives are more powerful and may catapult his emotions toward sexual

climax. Unless each understands the nature of these differing reactions, there can be misunderstanding and perhaps real trouble.
Teaching detailed information about sexual intercourse, in a
mixed group or in the church setting is not at all advisable. This
kind of material is best handled by parents who are mature and
prepared to do the job.

Still youth groups in the church present a wholesome setting for education in the Christian standards of sex relations.
There young people can learn from their peers as well as from
the adults, for much of the communication of sex attitudes must
take place in peer groups. Undoubtedly the young people help
one another to think things through. (It is of interest that educators no longer deplore the behind-the-fence sex talk of children because it enables them to discuss freely a difficult subject,
and later they can come to their parents for correction and revi-
sions.) Certainly there is no longer any reason for the church to
interpret in our Christian education only the spiritual side of
sex. Unless the Christian interpretation of sex is shown to be
both spiritual and physical, it is not true.

Facts about sex techniques are not unimportant and ought certainly to be accurate; but it is attitudes about sex that loom largest of all, and these we have seen are communicated very early
in life. Somehow children have sensed that there is something
mysterious about sex, and, in some families, that there is something evil here, even before they know what sex is. They begin
to pick up scattered bits about sex from movies, magazines, popular songs, radio serials, comic books, their friends, and their
family, and form opinions in early life. If in these same early
years, parents can get through to the child with rudimentary
facts about sexual anatomy and function before his opinions are
too set, or before this material has any emotional importance to
the youngster, a valuable lesson will have been learned. This
process is often considered to be touchy and embarrassing, but
only for the adult. Helen Parkhurst in *Exploring the Child's
World* (p. 138) wrote: "The ten-year-old daughter of an acquaintance of mine was told the facts of life very simply and
reassuringly by her father. When he had finished, the child said

with restraint: 'Thank you very much, Daddy, but I don't think I shall need that information for quite a long time.'"

The most direct channel to this educational goal again is the parents, and the church can work with and through them. The pastor in his ministry to young married couples can help them to formulate their own Christian attitudes toward sex, and can help them with vocabulary and definitions for teaching children. If in group discussion they review the ways to teach sex facts to their children, it also has the desirable result of improving their own relationships. Such teaching need not involve the organization of new classes or clubs, but can be introduced into adult groups and couples clubs that already exist.

The place of the church in such education is clear. Although some object to the fitness of such a program, it is obviously integral to Christian education as a part of our understanding of the creation and function of man. At an international conference of churchmen recently it was strongly stated: " If the Christian Church can say something decisively and significantly Christian about sex in the language of ordinary men and women, then it will be only a generation until Western Europe is Christian again."

The church that carries on a quiet, consistent program of sex education as a part of its Christian education program will find its young people better prepared for marriage and better fitted for family life. Teachers will be ready to answer questions about sex and reproduction as unemotionally as any other query, using correct scientific terms for organs and functions rather than some euphemistic evasion. The many good films, pamphlets, recordings, and books on this subject available from mental health associations will be geared into the total curriculum. And work with parents will include also this most vital segment of family life.

At present less than five per cent of our churches do anything significant in this field, and fewer than twenty states have school curriculums that include sex instruction. If Kinsey was correct in reporting that most men had formed their sex attitudes by age sixteen, attention to the need for early sex education cannot be given too soon.

From the early years upward, children in all their relationships need to be trained for family living: how to get along with parents, understand themselves, develop friendships, appreciate ideals, form standards for choosing a mate, and, later, know something of the God-given privilege of sex love in marriage. Where this kind of education has been planned, the young people are enthusiastic about its value; they later have a higher proportion of stable marriages, and they look back with gratitude upon the calm interpretation of sex life they have received. Any association of ministers co-operating with community leaders can do what has been done in Detroit, Toledo, Atlanta, and many other areas, and that is to plan such courses for parents as well as for their children, and to place this subject where it belongs — in the whole curriculum of Christian life.

Dating, Engagement, and Sex Ethics

Long before a young couple ever come to the pastor in premarital conferences, they have had to work through some momentous decisions about sex relationships. If the pastor is a particularly empathic counselor, trusted by his parishioners to keep a confidence and to counsel without scolding, young people will occasionally come to him with their questions about Christian conduct and sexual behavior. Even when they do not seek him out, the pastor in his preaching, teaching, calling, writing, and conversing has innumerable opportunities to help straighten out the tangled confusion of misinformation and misconduct in sex. It is fortunate that his pastoral office contains such opportunities, for a great many such tangles require straightening.

Greater toleration of sexual promiscuity is having its deleterious effect upon our young people. It is among their age group that the incidence of venereal disease increases, even while it is decreasing in the American population at large. It is among them also, school authorities report, that the sale of contraceptives has reached alarming proportions. In their high school sex clubs, found here and there across the country, they have subscribed to "the new morality" which Leslie Weatherhead notes is neither new nor moral.

Young people in our churches are found to be more resistant to sexual delinquency, but some of them too, as pastors can attest, find themselves in sexual tangles beyond their strength to combat. It would be miraculous if all of them withstood the claptrap of popular psychology that condemns " suppression " (discipline) and advocates " self-realization " (license). The late Fritz Künkel nailed down this psychological heresy: " Even some medical men have advised early and frequent sexual intercourse for adolescents, or masturbation as a substitute. Much talk about the evils of inhibition has persuaded a willing audience that self-gratification is the path to mental health. A medical prescription of this kind is a professional error which does inestimable harm. It rests on no foundation of worth, and cannot be supported by reference to any well-developed system of psychology. Those who advocate it have lost all understanding of the essential problem of human life: the development of the I into the we." (*What Do You Advise?* p. 197.)

Still the idea of sexual freedom crops out of countless novels of which this clever passage from *Thunder on the Left* (p. 175), by Christopher Morley, is only illustrative:

" As though down a long avenue of distance he saw her in the perspective of her life: an exquisite, gallant figure going about her brave concerns: so small and resolute in her single struggle with the world, and coming to his arms at last. He knew then that poets have not lied; that fairy tales are true; that life is hunger, and, for every emptiness, caters its own just food. Her mind that he had loved was tangled up with a body. Chastity was probably a much overrated virtue. For her sake, if she desired it, he was willing to make the heroic effort which is necessary to yield to temptation."

With such stimulation, contemporary young people and young adults cry for clarification of the issues in sexual morality and encouragement to stand by a defensible code. They are all too aware of their sex urges, and know the desire to experiment. They feel guilty, bewildered, and thwarted; and they require some realistic reassurance. When they talk it over frankly with the pastor, they frequently reveal that they don't so much want heavy petting; but the girls feel that unless they indulge in it the boys will have nothing to do with them; and the fellows confess that they believe that girls expect it. In this vicious cycle, they establish destructive patterns that may later exclude the mutuality necessary to marital adjustment, and perpetuate an infantile habit of seeking self-gratification.

This pitiful desire for popularity lies behind so much petting. Our young people need easy access to the kind of wise pastoral counseling that can aid them in building the ego strength that they lack. In their confusion they tend to feel that prohibition of their gratification amounts to senseless restraint. What they need instead is guidance to see that self-discipline is actually a contribution to personal growth and satisfaction. As long as they view sex as recreation or thrill activity, they remain too childish for marriage. The person who craves heavy petting may have been deprived of affection at home, or may have been under the hand of a domineering parent. If the pastor can help soon enough to correct the home situation, the pressure for petting can also lift.

However, it will be recalled that Kinsey's specious philosophizing upon his study of female sex behavior allowed one to conclude that premarital sex experience somehow better qualified a person for good marriage relations. Dr. Edmund Bergler criticized this allegation severely, noting that exactly the opposite is indicated by clinically observable facts, that prolonged heavy petting actually militates against satisfactory marriage adjustment. Extensive experimentation with sex is characteristic of neurotics and abnormal personalities who hope that pseudo sex satisfaction on a trial and error basis will lead to something better. In such encounters the love element is entirely ignored to indulge a physical relationship. " In short," writes Dr. Bergler, " sex is more than a matter of ' practice.' It is not like learning a new sport. The grave psychological dangers involved in Kinsey's half-hinting, half-advisory summary, though tempered with stylistic caution, are too great to be overlooked." (*Kinsey's Myth of Female Sexuality*, p. 44.)

Young men and women who have avoided promiscuous petting throughout their dating experience nevertheless come into a new problem at the time of engagement. Now they feel that they have made their choice, that they will soon be " as good as married," and that the mere ceremony of the wedding is all that remains between them and this one last realization. Society does not object if they now have joint budget plans, pledges of undying love, or discussions about draperies and furniture. Why should they deny themselves that one experience in sexual mutuality for which they crave? Engagement is a time, as Prof. L. M. Terman says, " during which the idea of marriage with this particular mate is being explored as a working hypothesis." That such sexual participation may lead to a broken engagement rather than to marriage is known to ministers but inconceivable to lovers. That unwanted pregnancy may result is demonstrated by the countless marriages in which a baby is born too soon after the nuptials. That an auto accident, premature death, or a change of mind can result in losing this mate does not even seem possible to them. But to the observer less emotionally involved these are facts to consider.

How great the weight of decision is concerning premarital intercourse has been revealed in a study published by *Marriage and Family Living* (February, 1954, p. 51). There it was shown that one prominent advice column in a national magazine had to deal with the problem of premarital sex intercourse in 52 per cent of the letters received (3,371 letters in one year's time). At one time the three terrors of conception, infection, or detection were enough to frighten people into moral living, but these sanctions no longer hold much power. Religious influence carries some weight, but it takes more than routine devotions to protect the powerfully sexed person from temptation.

The real picture of premarital coitus is not a romantic one. Clandestine meetings, often in some motel or automobile, fall far short of the glamorous vision of soft lights and music in which movies and novels portray affairs. In fact, Robert O. Blood, who has made extensive studies in dating patterns of university students, reports that students find that " going the limit" and romance are likely to be mutually exclusive (*Anticipating Your Marriage*).

Premarital sex experience sometimes prevents the very process its proponents claim for it — a growing together in trust and understanding. Instead, sex can become the expression of hostility, aggression, and anxiety. Rather than working toward a good adjustment in marriage, this experience then moves in exactly the opposite direction. Sexual compatibility, after all, is not the result of mastering techniques or playing erotic games; a good sexual adjustment grows out of a marriage of mature personalities. Until the churches can work more realistically in helping their people attain personal maturity, they will be doing little to help them find sexual satisfaction no matter how many books on sex harmony are circulated from the church library.

The Church must reiterate its convictions: that sexual union without moral union is grossly inadequate, and that sexual discipline is a *sine qua non* both in marriage and before. Sex is a way to mutual discovery; truly in this relationship a man comes to *know* his wife and he discovers something of his own masculinity in that act. It is hardly necessary for young couples to experiment with sex to learn what they already realize, viz., that they are sexually attracted to each other. What is necessary is that in the whole educational program of the Church they be helped to realize the essential nature of personal development toward Christian maturity. From this strong marriage is built, even when sexual satisfactions are few.

Objective observers with no doctrinal ax to grind have reached conclusions that support the stand of the Church on sex ethics. The medical researchers in *The Peckham Experiment* concluded that unchastity " far from having any use in assisting in making an apposite selection of a mate is biologically a dangerous procedure liable to confuse the developing specificity of each partner. For we must recall the fact that any ' foreign' or promiscuously introduced substance given in small doses tends to create reactionary allergy, or anaphylaxis. It is thus likely that in promiscuous intercourse we shall find that the *specific* quality of each participant is being blurred, defaced, and worn down to accomanality. . . . Thus the manliness of adolescent chastity and the womanliness of adolescent virginity may well be no mere ideal of moral philosophy; it may be the expression of nature's discriminative behavior in furthering the genus of *homo sapiens,* his individuality and his uniqueness." (*The Peckham Experiment; A Study in the Living Structure of Society,* by Innes H. Pearse and Lucy H. Crocker, p. 234.) Society gives little opportunity to try out sexual relationships before marriage, and even if it did, such trials would rarely eventuate in strong marriages. Sylvanus M. Duvall, writing in *Men, Women and Morals* (p. 284), claims that he began his study with an open mind and permissive attitude, expecting that "further study would swing me farther in this direction. Somewhat to my surprise, I found that the more critically and carefully I examined the evidence, the more conservative I became." He landed at the point where any objective study must, taking account of what Frederick L. Robertson used to call "the grand old landmarks of morality." Without their help, we lose our way.

The Premarital Interview

Much more is understood today about marriage and its breakdown than ever before, but marriage preparation still has not been reduced to a science. Each couple must be met on their own terms and must have reinterpreted just for them what Christian marriage is. This is a custom-fitted operation, highly personal and often difficult. While it is possible within certain broad areas to predict what marital harmony they may have, the well-known marriage prediction scales are not intended to be accurate within one thousandth of an inch measurements. Marriage prediction tests were pioneered by Ernest Burgess and Leonard Cottrell after they discovered that it was possible to predict a convict's chances for rehabilitation after prison parole. They then tried a similar set of intelligence and psychological tests on marriage partners to predict marital success. Their two studies, together with another version developed by L. M. Terman, attempt to discover what makes marriage successful, what personality factors are associated with such success, and how these can be translated into a prediction for any given couple. The questions deal with finances, religion, recreation, selection of friends, intimate relations, table manners, feelings of unhappiness, and many more categories.

It was found that an active church relationship for both members of the couple was correlated with happy marriage. The studies showed that if both parties are from the same faith, and if they have a church wedding, their chances of stable family life are greater. They discovered that if a couple had determination to make marriage succeed, would use their intelligence to think through their problems, and were adjusted in a relationship of love, their chances for marital happiness were very high. But the most arresting conclusion of these tests was that in happy marriages there was a recurrent pattern of family stability recapitulated generation after generation. Clearly, happiness runs in families.

If it were really possible to submit a couple to a set of psychological tests and then to predict accurately their chances for marital felicity within a fraction of a percentile, pastors would have no work to do in premarital guidance. The whole process could be run through an IBM machine. But prediction tests are not that cold, not that certain. Their real contribution for those who use them is to uncover areas that need some additional understanding, and to serve as talking points about anticipated problems and plans. The tests developed by Burgess, Cottrell, and Terman are not the only ones in the field. Gilbert Appelhof of Berea, Ohio, has designed a test to help high school young people select a mate. The American Institute of Family Relations makes standard use of the Johnson Temperament Analysis. Other counselors select from the wealth of testing programs the Bernreuter test, the Minnesota Multiphasic or California personality tests, the schedule of the Marriage Council of Philadelphia, or the Guilford-Zinn temperament survey. If the pastor chooses to use one of these, he will select the one that best suits his purpose, and then supplement it with his own counseling methods.

Book dealers tell about one enterprising publisher who ran an advertisement offering a book " from which the young can learn, not those things which are usually told before marriage, but those things which they ought to know." The ad emphasized that the book would not be sold over the counter but would be mailed in a plain wrapper to any address from which an order came. The result was sensational. Two thousand orders a week arrived from young women and men who wished to be initiated into such knowledge. What they received for their money, however, was astonishing to all customers. It turned out to be a cookbook, and an item of publisher's overstock, at that.

When one customer sued the publisher for fraudulent advertising, the judge opined: " To my mind cooking is precisely what a young man or woman needs to know before marriage. If you were ashamed to see the book before buying, that was your affair. What you wanted may not have been quite so edifying as what you got."

Yet there are a great many things the prospective bride and groom need to know prior to marriage, and cooking is but one of them. The tragedy of couples going into marriage half informed and unprepared for the great venture ahead of them is evident to anyone who reads the daily slate of divorce decrees in the press. What is more pathetic is that some of these marital mishaps might have been prevented by the Church and the clergymen if they had been more alert. The Church has a sacred duty in this matter. In its sanctuary the knot of most marriages is tied. The Church, therefore, is obligated to make sure that the knot is tied as firmly as possible. This means premarital education.

Even if it is a last-minute, catch-as-catch-can procedure, the premarital interview still has some commendable points. It is far better, of course, to have a continuing educational program that helps to prepare young people for marriage, and then leads them up to a series of premarital conferences in plenty of time for the wedding. Premarital conferences vary greatly in quantity and in quality among pastors. Some conduct one such conference. Others go into six sessions. More important than the number of sessions is what happens in them. The pastor who is friendly and encouraging and helps his young couples to see the importance of preparation and insight before approaching marriage may do far more than all the tests devised to search out their readiness. He must help them over the idea that marriage is something that happens naturally, for which they need no special qualifications except having reached the age of consent.

This, however, is a counsel of perfection best fulfilled when both parties of the couple have long been members of the same church and open to the pastor's ministry. In cases where the bridegroom comes from a distant place just one or two days prior to the wedding, or where the couple are out-of-towners come back to the family church for the ceremony, it is obvious that premarital counseling opportunity has to be cut to fit the occasion. Still the conscientious pastor can do much within these limits.

A common yet very effective device used by many pastors is to read through the wedding service itself with the young couple who are about to be married. Point by point he can discuss the inferences of the liturgy with them, and they will find that almost every topic of importance is suggested. This has the advantage of being an educational technique that gives a more-than-human reference. God is in marriage. To enable the couple to realize that God is made known in their unity and that his blessing is upon marriage is at once encouraging and sound. If care is taken to instruct the couple before the proposed wedding, many a difficulty can be uncovered and corrected. Sometimes a delay in plans will be indicated, and the pastor may have to call attention to that. Occasionally premarital counseling has put the brakes on a hasty venture into matrimony and has forced the couple to consider their leap. The pastor dare not take for granted that the possession of a marriage license proves that a couple are ready.

When the couple first come to the minister, their immediate questions have to do with the wedding ceremony itself. The resulting interviews are eased if this question can be settled in every possible detail at that time: date, type of service, music, rehearsal, bridal party, flowers, whether the reception is to be held in the church, and so on. Meeting with both parties of the couple at the same time gives the pastor a chance to observe their relationships, to watch for signs of disagreement, of domination, of immaturity. Conflict between lovers prior to matrimony will probably increase in intensity afterward, and the pastor will be alert to this.

It is advisable then to see each of them alone, the other meanwhile waiting outside with a book or pamphlet on marriage. In these separate interviews strict confidence should be stressed so that each will speak of attitudes toward the wedding, concerns about the other person, feelings about prospective in-laws, anxieties about marital relations, and, if there was one, circumstances of any previous marriage. To help them reveal their innermost feelings in these individual conferences is important to their self-understanding, and may open into further, needed counseling. When they have each been interviewed alone, the pastor ought to see them together again briefly, review the dates and plans simply to clarify any misunderstanding, and then after a brief prayer dismiss them until the next interview. For the intervening period, they might be given a book to read together, such as: *Harmony in Marriage,* by Leland Foster Wood; *Education for Marriage,* by James A. Peterson; *This Man and This Woman,* by Frederick W. Brink; *Looking Toward Marriage,* by Johnson, Randolph, and Pixley; *The Marriage Handbook,* by Judson T. and Mary G. Landis; *When You Marry,* by Evelyn M. Duvall and Reuben L. Hill; *Sex in Marriage,* by Ernest R. and Gladys M. Groves; and one of a quite different nature, *A Diary of Private Prayer,* by John Baillie.

For the second and following interviews, it is helpful to have a check list of questions for discussion. Some of these will have grown out of the first session. Others are fairly standard and cover such topics as: How do you handle conflicts? Are your parents in complete understanding and approval of the wedding? How will you handle your finances? What are your plans for children? Where do you expect to live? What kind of home do you expect to establish? What will be your religious practice in church, in family worship? What interests have you in common? What interests do you have exclusively? When you quarrel, how do you usually make up? Do you know all that you need to know about sexual relations? Have you had a physical examination?

Most physicians do not conduct a complete physical examination of the bride unless it is specifically requested. But an examination ought to include not only the required blood test but also a pelvic examination, instruction about contraception, and the answering of any questions about which she is concerned. The pastor would do well to locate those doctors in the community who will perform such examinations, and recommend such persons to the young couples. This arrangement is superior to the blanket advice to "consult your family physician," because sometimes this kind of examination is not his dish of tea at all. A physician in a Midwestern city who has specialized in this service conducts a general class on marriage one night each week. Then he sees the persons individually after he has discussed general information with all of them together.

The degree to which a minister ought to discuss sexual relationships with the young couples is a matter of wide debate. That he ought certainly to stress the Christian interpretation of sex standards is generally agreed; that he might also teach that our faith finds nothing shameful about marital relations is less subscribed by some. But when it comes to details about coitus and contraception, clergymen seem to discuss only just as far as they can and still feel comfortable. Some use the *Sex Knowledge Inventory* designed by Gelolo McHugh of Durham, North Carolina. Those who institute the use of so intimate a form as this are advised first to discuss it with their official board and to be sure that the members of the board have a complete understanding of the process. Whether the pastor uses such a device or not, he will be helpful in interpreting sex as emotional warmth and not just as animal instinct, in assuring couples that God created our sex and has a purpose therein, and in reminding them that sex combines the physical and the spiritual in us. The pastor will sometimes uncover some attitude or condition that needs correction and will make a referral to the gynecologist or urologist who can be of help. And if he is lucky, he may be the means of aiding the couple to have a happy and sensible honeymoon rather than the trying, restless experience it becomes for so many.

But all is not accomplished in premarital interviews. The pastor has a carry-through with his people, and he can continue to

educate them from pulpit and pastoral calls long after they have
established their home. Some pastors call on a couple and lead
them in family worship soon after their return from a honeymoon. It may be that then they will hear him say things they
missed altogether when with starry-eyed bewilderment they were
thinking instead about flowers, rings, and ushers. One enterprising pastor organizes little groups of newly married couples
into home discussion fellowships.

There is enough truth in the platitude that families who pray
together stay together, to encourage every bit of family worship
help that can be given. Leslie Weatherhead, writing in *The Mastery of Sex Through Psychology and Religion* (p. 86), said:

" When I was younger and bolder I used to extract a promise from
every couple that I married. I used to say that I would marry them
only on condition that every night they said a prayer together, even if
it were only this: ' O God, keep us true to one another and to thee.'
I have since come to think that it was presumptuous on my part to
demand this, but if I were a millionaire I think I would give a wedding present to every couple I married. It should be one of those
prie-dieux at which two can kneel together side by side. And I think
I would ask them to use it every night, because, obviously, you cannot keep up an estrangement with your wife, you cannot allow things
that separate to do any harm, you cannot become selfish and over-
bearing, you cannot tolerate an interloper, if, night after night, you
are praying with her at the feet of God. What God so constantly
joins together nothing can put asunder."

The pastor cannot in the few weeks before a wedding turn a
bad marriage prospect into a good one. But he will be able to take
two uncertain people, poised on the threshold of life's greatest
venture, and teach them what God created for them in marriage.
He can show them as Antoine de Saint-Exupéry wrote in *Wind,
Sand and Stars:* " Life has taught us that love does not consist
in gazing at each other, but in looking outward together in the
same direction. There is no comradeship except from union in
the same high effort. That is the building of a Christian home."
(Quoted from *Making Your Marriage Succeed,* by Theodore F.
Adams, p. 61.)

Special Problems for the Pastor

1. *Teen-age Marriages.* Census figures of 1950 reveal that there were more than one million married teen-agers that year, but the proportion has increased markedly since then. The times have been propitious for earlier marriage and the country's prosperity has made jobs plentiful and teen-age marriage economically feasible. The new enthusiasm for familism in our culture has reached into younger ages, causing them to seek matrimony, and at the same time has made parents and school authorities more tolerant of the idea. Compulsory military training has sped some couples into marriage, partly because it has lightened the financial burden slightly, and because, as always, the strain of anticipated separation encourages decision to marry.

The prognosis for these teen-age marriages, however, is not so favorable. When requested to marry a pair of teen-agers, the pastor will reflect on such figures as: the divorce rate of teen-age marriages is six times that of people married in their thirties; the 1950 census shows that over 24,000 " women " between the ages of 14 and 19 are divorced. Financial and other problems tend to perpetuate themselves in marriage because educational preparation may have been cut short by the early wedding. Too often teen-agers marry for reasons that are hardly propitious for marital stability: for sexual satisfaction alone, for fun, out of infatuation, because of rebelliousness against parents, or in order to escape a home relationship they dislike.

Obvious to any pastor is the need for earlier education for marriage. It will hardly suffice to schedule studies in marriage preparation for those in their twenties if by then they have already been divorced. Much of our effort in this subject has been too little and too late. As David Mace says, " If we allowed ships to put to sea in the same state of unreadiness as we allow nice young people to embark upon married life, no one would be in the least surprised to see many of them founder before they got far from shore " (*Marriage: The Art of Lasting Love,* p. 186). Today's churches are going to have to inaugurate educational features they have not previously considered. Some churches in South Carolina and Georgia sponsor pregnancy classes for expectant mothers. Group counseling techniques are used with young engaged couples in one Chicago parish. A pastor in a Kansas church distributes notes and reviews about books, pamphlets, and articles that prove helpful to young people. But most common of all, and in many ways most helpful, is the continuing social program available in thousands of church youth groups that helps young people to come together under wholesome circumstances, to meet one another and to date.

One additional type of education, seldom mentioned in this connection, is the conduct of the unmarried minister himself. As a young man, under theological orders, or perhaps already ordained and serving as a pastor, he has heavy influence upon the dating mores of his young friends. If he himself is not considerate or honest about flirtation and courtship, what can be expected of his parishioners? One parish, located within the shadow of a great theological seminary, have the custom of hiring students each year to assist in their church work. They like these young men, find them zealous and personable, but sometimes have had occasion to ask, "Have they never seen a girl before?" While we are building into the spirit of our seminary experience a respect and enthusiasm for marriage, we might also be building a discipline for premarital conduct. The problem is not that of morals, but one of mature relationships, a field in which the clergy should be specialists.

2. *Mixed Marriages.* Rare is the minister these days who does not have to cope with the issue of mixed marriage in his church membership. Matrimony across religious lines has grown so common that in some Roman Catholic parishes as many as 40 per cent of the young people wed outside their faith. The gradually increasing conversion rate to Judaism (about two thousand converts a year) is almost entirely the result of intermarriage between Jew and Gentile.

Matrimony across racial lines has been on the increase since World War II when American GI's began to bring home Japanese brides by the thousands. Accurate statistics are impossible to find, but there is reason to believe that Negro-white marriages are more frequent at present. Marriages across these lines of

Church denomination, nationality, class, and culture will continue as peoples move across land and sea with greater ease and encounter one another at closer range in our ever more crowded cities. City living, widening tolerances, increased mobility, better economic conditions, and greater social freedom have opened the way to more and more intermarriage.

The question always follows: What are the chances for success in mixed marriages? Evidence is conflicting, but not many advocates of marriage across society's boundaries are able to advise couples to go ahead without adding a series of provisions. One Protestant wife of a Roman Catholic husband looks back at her experience and encourages other couples of mixed faiths to consider marriage only *if* they can agree before the wedding to understand and tolerate each other's faith, establish sensible standards for child-rearing and stick by them, work out satisfactory relationships with both sets of in-laws, and leave room for future adjustments. Reuben L. Hill in *Families Under Stress* finds that an interfaith marriage adjusted well to war separation and reunion *if* the couple were mature and loving. Interracial marriages may work out *if* the community is willing to allow to such families their freedom and to extend friendship.

However, other voices also point out the hazards. Mixed marriages of every sort have a statistically poorer chance for stability than those in which man and wife share the same background. Landis and Landis found that where both spouses agree on religion 65 per cent have very happy marriages; where they do not, less than 33 per cent are very happy. An intensive survey of one Roman Catholic parish on the Atlantic Coast showed that " the chances of divorce are more than twice as great in the case of mixed marriages." The split-ups of veterans and their war brides from other cultures have reached such alarming proportions that some military chaplains unequivocally discourage all such weddings.

Perhaps the clue to the problem is to be found in the motive behind the mixed marriage, for it appears that the motives in a mixed marriage are also mixed. The representative from the more stable majority group may be seeking to establish a position of superiority he has never before enjoyed. One from a minority or disadvantaged culture may be acting out his dependency needs and seeking a foothold in status to compensate for a cultural blow. Someone with a messiah complex may want a mixed marriage in order to defy convention and atone for the injustice his group has visited upon another. Such complex motivations suggest that when a mixed marriage is broken, it may be more because of psychological and personality difficulties than the cultural or religious differences that are so easily documented in statistics.

The pastor's experience with mixed marriages is most frequently a case where a member of his flock plans to marry a Roman Catholic. When a man and woman of these different religious backgrounds are married, their religious interest is not doubled. It doesn't work that way. Quite the opposite — their religious activity is likely to wane and perish. It is estimated that more than half of the men in mixed marriages and more than a third of the women drop their church contacts altogether. This is no accident, for many couples of mixed religions find it easier to avoid tension if they omit references to matters of faith and its practice.

In recent years intermarriage of Roman Catholics and Protestants has been increasing. One popular magazine has recently polled its readers and found that the majority of them were tolerant of these unions. Both the Roman Catholics and the Protestants have sought to stanch the flow of couples through the intermarriage gates, but without noticeable success to date. As a result the Church must make clear to the young people and to the membership as a whole what is involved in the interfaith marriage. We know that the Roman Catholic Church will exact a heavy pledge from the non-Catholic in an antenuptial agreement to make sure that nothing is done to discourage the Roman Catholic partner in his religious practice and to ascertain that any and all children born to the union will be brought up as Roman Catholics. Unless the procedure is carried out along lines that the hierarchy has decreed, the Roman Catholic may be excommunicated. If the Protestant signs the antenuptial agreement, he capitulates to an arrangement which for him is basically immoral, for he has committed a generation yet unborn to a religious faith he cannot approve. As James A. Pike bluntly states in *If You Marry Outside Your Faith:* "While his church may not 'excommunicate' him in a formal sense, he should feel barred from communion with God — through the sacrament or otherwise — until he can work out some solution as to the matter of repentance for sin. So in essence both parties are in the same situation, or, to put it in another way, one of the parties is in a fix either way the matter is decided" (p. 107). Thus the Protestant passes on to others one of life's most precious responsibilities, the spiritual nurture of his children. The heart-tearing experiences that can result when a child is taken for Baptism to a strange church in the arms of godparents, or when evening prayers become exclusive, are something that must be felt to be appreciated. One mother attests, "Spiritually, I have a constant loneliness, not because my husband and sons are Catholics, but because they cannot be given an unbiased explanation of and understanding for Protestantism." From the very first when the wedding begins as a second-class service without prayers, benediction, or religious allusion by the priest, through to the confirmation of children in Catholicism, this kind of family life is divisive. Yet the Roman Catholic Church remains adamant. Father John J. Kane states their case in *Marriage and the Family* (p. 152): "The Roman Catholic Church is the one true Church. There is no such thing as equality of religions from the Catholic standpoint. Therefore, to have offspring reared in another faith is a catastrophe, since it denies to the persons for whom one has the greatest love the grace of the sacraments and solaces of Roman Catholicism in life and death. It means that one permits his children to be reared in religious error. Such words may appear harsh to non-Catholics, but truth is objective. . . . No non-Catholic is compelled to marry a Catholic, but if one wishes to do so, he does it knowing very well what responsibilities such a marriage places upon him."

Pastors have developed a variety of stratagems to combat the encroachment of Catholicism into the church by means of wedding bells. One minister requests young couples anticipating this step to talk with certain married couples who have already taken it, and he finds that those who speak from the validity of experience can often say more direct and relevant things than ever he could. In many instances, this conversation has meant a turning point in wedding plans. Another pastor holds a Communion service for the Protestant party plus family and friends on the same day as the wedding. He reports that this sacrament has eased the tension of brides who had always hoped to be married in their own church, and that the bride's parents find a great weight lifted from their own hearts. One pastor reports that he has devised his own antenuptial statement, and asks couples of mixed faiths to sign it. Another pastor, located in a town heavily populated with Roman Catholics, offers an annual course on the subject of Catholicism and marriage to young people in the church. It is enlightening for his young people to learn that the Roman Catholics who are married outside their Church are considered (in the words of the Catholic Information Center) "invalidly married, are living in sin, and stand in constant danger of damnation." This pastor's method is the most promising measure because it is prevention. Our young people would not be marrying Roman Catholics (and sometimes leaving thereby to unite with the Roman Catholic Church) if they had been warned away from the first date. After they're in love, it's too late.

Marriage across racial lines in these times of tension represents a very different problem. Often these are in-faith unions against which no moral or religious objection can be raised except that which arises from prudence. The World Council of Churches concluded its 1954 meeting at Evanston with a provocative message on race relations. In it the World Council said: " While . . . [we] can find in the Bible no clear justification or condemnation of intermarriage, . . . [we] cannot approve any law against racial or ethnic intermarriage. Marriage involves primarily a decision between two individuals before God which goes beyond the jurisdiction of state or culture. There is no evidence that the children of such marriages are inherently inferior, and any treat-

ment of them as such should be condemned." Nor are we alone
in such a statement. Joseph Doherty in *Moral Problems of Interracial Marriage,* published by the Catholic University of America,
states that from their point of view the natural right to marry includes also the right to marry the person of one's own choice,
and to marry a particular person regardless of race.

The question in a Negro-white marriage has little to do with
their moral right to marry. The real question is how well they
are suited to each other, and how they can live in the community
they choose. As suggested above, their motives may be influenced by psychological factors not connected at all with racism
or tolerance. Certainly if ordinary couples are in need of the type
of premarital counseling discussed earlier in this chapter so much
the more will a Negro-white combination require careful counseling. As our churches improve their racial integration and more
Negroes cross the color line, the challenge of this kind of premarital counseling may well increase. For the consideration of a
clergyman entering such a task, the 1948 Statement on Interracial
Marriage by the Committee on Church and Race of the Congregational Christian Churches is apropos:

" Special attention will need to be given, when the marriage is between persons of different racial ancestries, to the emotional maturity
and the spiritual resources of the two principals. This should include
consideration of how successful the parents are likely to be in adjusting themselves and in preparing their children to adjust to the
discriminations and tensions in which they will inevitably be involved because of the sub-Christian atmosphere of present-day United
States. Thus, in most cases, parties to an interracial marriage and
their children have relatively greater difficulty in being accepted
socially by one or both racial groups involved.

" God is ' no respecter of persons.' ' He looks not upon the outward appearance but upon the heart.' ' God hath made of one blood
all nations of men.' Hence, neither color nor racial ancestry in itself
presents a real barrier to fellowship or to marriage. Race is relevant
to marriage only in so far as our unchristian color distinctions make
an interracial marriage more difficult than marriage within a given
racial group. Scientific research does not sustain the frequently stated
opinion that crossbreeding between persons of different stocks (i.e.,

black and white or yellow and white) results in biological deteriora-
tion. Moreover, the evidence is overwhelming that, over the past ten
to twenty thousand years at least, members of all three distinguish-
able racial stocks (black, white, or yellow) have been mixing their
'blood' until it is no longer possible to find a 'pure' or 'unmixed'
race. See article 'Race Mixture' by Melville J. Nerskovits in Vol.
XIII, *Encyclopaedia of the Social Sciences;* and the book *Characteristics of the American Negro,* Otto Klineberg, ed."

The Wedding

Old Testament accounts of marriage include no wedding ceremony. A contract arrangement of betrothal was made, the bride
went to the bridegroom's tent as a ritualistic indication of her
willingness to marry, and a wedding feast followed. That was
that. The laws and customs of Judaism were impressively strict
about faithfulness and honor in marriage, and their unions were
generally permanent. As time went on, more ritual and ceremony were added to this event until it included a variety of
bizarre and complex customs. Some Roman Catholic brides once
wore a red veil to symbolize natural love, and the groom lifted
it and put it over his own head also during the early part of the
wedding. In the Coptic wedding, bride and groom both wear
crowns and the priest anoints the couple with oil to signify how
God crowns this couple as a royal pair and blesses their home-to-
be. In Russian services until the beginning of this century, the
brothers of the bride staged a mock battle with the family of the
groom, evidently a vestigial remnant of those days in which wives
were captured and wrested from their clans.

In American Protestantism, however, we have seen ceremonies
that are even more bizarre: weddings performed on roller skates,
in submarines, and on television shows. In the Christian ministry
such a travesty has no place. The minister has always an obligation to make a wedding a godly ceremony, and to recognize it
for what it is, a worship service of the church community. For
this reason it is advisable to hold the wedding, no matter how
small the party may be, in the church rather than in home,
manse, or garden. This means that a wedding in the church is
open to the entire church, and not only to those who have re-

ceived an engraved invitation, for this is the church at worship. In such a philosophy there is a real place for the growing custom of presenting a brief address on marriage during the service, wherein the pastor proclaims the meaning of the Word in regard to Christian marriage. There is also good reason for considering inclusion of the sacrament of Holy Communion as the couple acknowledge their oneness with fellow members of this mystical body, the Church, and recognize their new estate in relation to the entire company of the faithful. It is well, however, to recall that Communion is a congregational experience, and not a private affair for the bride and groom as in Roman Catholic tradition.

Gradually the unfortunate practice of seating the groom's friends on one side and the bride's on the other is passing away. The feud concept of the wedding, from which this stems, has no place in modern church life. In fact, there is much to commend the newer custom of having the parents of both bride and groom stand with them through the early part of the service, rather than just the bride's father. The artificial division of families and friends in the wedding service is as archaic as that ugly query put to the congregation: "If there be any here present who knows any just cause why they may not lawfully be joined in marriage, I require him now to make it known, or ever after to hold his peace." Conscientious premarital counseling will have made such a checkup question unnecessary.

While we are at it, there is another outdated custom connected with the performance of weddings. That is the expectation of a fee by the officiating minister. Today's salary schedules in most denominations make it inappropriate for the clergyman to hold out his hand for some gratuity at times of special services. And if the salary is inadequate, a frank recognition by pastor and officers that he ought to be able to live off his salary independent of tips, and to perform all his ministerial duties as a part of his vocation without free-lancing, often has the salutary effect of bringing about a salary review.

Many churches today have a set of instructions for weddings, available in brochure form, to explain the nature of the service and the regulations of the church. Too often these simply tell of rules concerning decoration of the sanctuary, standards of music, and discipline of commercial photographers. In some brochures, however, standards are set forth concerning the schedule of premarital interviews and rehearsals, the nature of Christian marriage, the Church law about marriage, and appropriate conduct of the congregation at the wedding service. An excellent statement of this kind is distributed by the Trinity Episcopal Church of Oxford, Ohio, under the title of " Marriage, Weddings, and the Christian Faith." Wedding etiquette is a matter of great import to most bridal parties, and it ought not to be neglected. Helpful information on the order of events, what is expected in shared expenses, where the party should enter and stand can be found in such books as Sylvanus M. Duvall's *Before You Marry* and James Hine's *Your Wedding Workbook*. To these the individual minister will add his own standards about the sacred nature of marriage, the counseling sessions, the rehearsal (does it begin with prayer?), the service itself, and the way that records are to be completed.

Occasions arise when a pastor knows that he ought not to marry a couple. Premarital counseling will uncover conditions that may not make a Christian marriage possible. Since the pastor's reason for marrying at all is to help establish a Christian home, he will not marry those who frankly avow that they will practice sexual freedom outside of marriage, or those who plan to marry but never to allow children to enter this union, or those who, hard upon the issuance of a divorce decree, wish to marry the very person who figured in making the divorce inevitable. If the pastor has already established his own severance from the customary wedding fee, he is singularly able to turn down opportunities to marry those whose troth in good conscience he cannot plight. Freedom from fee also makes his voice more authoritative in scheduling premarital interviews, rehearsals, and conduct of the wedding party. So insidious is our tendency to rationalize desires that unless we are disinterested in anticipated income from the event, we may make exception to our standards and persuade ourselves that we have acted right.

The marriage of intoxicated couples, hurried weddings of furloughed soldiers, across-the-state-line marriages of runaway youngsters, eloping lovers who avoid parental disapproval: all these are eagerly welcomed by the wedding traffickers, some of whom are justices of the peace, magistrates, and village clerks, and some of whom are also ill-advised and often poorly educated clergymen. Lower standards of wedding services have become so common in some areas with their " wedding chapels " and " complete services " that it should surprise no one to find soon someone opening a drive-in marriage mart patterned after the newer banks where those who do business need not leave their automobile.

This is not to say that the service performed by a civil magistrate is invalid. In many countries, every couple must be married by an officer of the state and any church service that follows is an extra for the religiously inclined. The Massachusetts Bay Colony even prohibited marriage by clergymen and insisted that only civil magistrates could perform this function. Yet many a church couple married by some mayor or judge later wish that they could have had a church wedding, and they feel cheated by a premature and now regretted decision. There is for them a provision by which a civil marriage can be blessed. In most cases this ceremony is almost identical to the wedding service except that in the vows where a pastor would ask, " Do you take this man to be your husband? " etc., it is changed to read, " Do you acknowledge this man to be your wedded husband? " The prayers, the ring ceremony, the benediction can be identical; and a grateful couple often feel that there is an added significance to their marriage because this time they have acknowledged God's part in it.

Wedding music, like the ceremony itself, should be an act of worship. Such tonal abominations as " Indian Love Call," " Because," and " I Love You Truly," or the Roman Catholic " Ave Maria," have no more place in our wedding services than a football cheer has at Sunday morning worship. Most of these musical errors occur in the solos that creep into the service; and many of them could be avoided by use of the congregational singing of appropriate hymns, such as "O Love Divine and Golden," "Lead Us, Heavenly Father, Lead Us," or "Love Divine, All Loves Excelling." But there is also the unhallowed tradition of using the *Lohengrin* music as a processional; this stems from an opera marriage which according to the libretto was anything but happy. Better by far are *Wedding Cantata No. 196,* by Johann Sebastian Bach; *Nuptial March in E Major,* by A. Guilmant; and *Marche Nuptial,* by L. Ganne.

Futile as the attempt may be, the pastor still is obligated to encourage families to exercise due economy and to avoid showy weddings. It is possible for a wedding service to turn into a display instead of worship. Expensive floral decorations, huge suppers and receptions, and special attention to the prestige of the occasion can overshadow the solemn vows and the religious service that is taking place. It is to be hoped that along with the newer emphasis on counseling that has as its aim the building of a stable marital relationship, there will also grow up a concern to keep Christian wedding services simple and worshipful. The certificate of marriage given by the East Harlem Protestant Parish places the emphasis where it belongs — upon God's place in the marriage. The certificate is headed by the words from I John 4:7: "Beloved, let us love one another: for love is of God; and every one that loveth is born of God, and knoweth God."

6

CHRISTIAN MARRIAGE
AND MARRIAGE COUNSELING

Marriage is popular because it
combines the maximum of temptation
with the minimum of opportunity. — Bernard Shaw.

Ever flying in the face of popular mythology, the Church persists in the apparently ridiculous notion that marriage is not simply a *Liebestraum* but an institution established by God for the welfare and happiness of mankind. For many people this is difficult to comprehend, and the pastor finds himself repeating this conviction in preaching, in teaching, in counseling. Our clue to the divine purpose of married love is found in the Genesis story of creation. God had set in order the flora and fauna of the primitive world, and then climaxed it in making man. But because it was not good for man to be alone, we are told, woman was also created. They were created for relationship with each other, as well as with their God whose image they have always borne. From the very beginning when they were made male and female, they were fitted for co-humanity. Created as persons of infinite worth, they were children of God. It is from this faith that our understanding of marriage begins. Dr. Kinsey's biological bias does not help us understand more than the coital and reproductive functions. The romantic viewpoint does not get us past the glorification of eros in marriage, remarriage, and still more remarriage. Sigmund Freud has not aided us to see beyond the conscious and unconscious drives that operate in our libido. "For Freud, man was entirely existence," William Graham Cole notes; " the inner intuition that one is somehow more than and better than the anguished conflicts and tragic missteps out of which the fabric of daily life is woven were ascribed by Freud either to illusion or to the work of an inflated super-ego " (*Sex in Christianity and Psychoanalysis,* p. 298).

Beginning with a different point of view, the Bible tells of God's creation of man and woman and how they were brought together into one flesh. It does not tell that each was half a person before this, and that they became whole only when they were wedded. This is the only mathematical sum known where one plus one equals one. Each is a completely whole individual prior to marriage; and yet when they come into this unitive relationship, a greater oneness is achieved. Such is the paradox of matrimony which has been written into our creation. Behind wisecracks about " the better half " is an old Platonic idea that a single person is but half a being until he finds his other fraction in marriage. Not so in Christian thought. For us, the unmarried woman or man is just as human, just as much a person, as the married. Their psychosexual development has shaped their personalities as surely as anyone's. Their glands secrete sex hormones too, aiding their femininity or masculinity. They also live full lives.

The basis of Christian marriage is not romantic love. At least it is not that love known as eros, and this is a truth hard for modern young people to take. Emil Brunner, who pulls no punches about the romantic illusion in marriage, bluntly writes: " Where marriage is based on love all is lost from the very outset." Marriage is too high and demanding an obligation for individuals to uphold its promises on the mere strength of their devotion to each other. Such devotion may be no deeper than what Leland Foster Wood has called " cardiac-respiratory love," a type touched off when two persons respond because their sexes are different and they have not yet discovered each other. Romantic love in our culture receives a great deal more attention than it deserves; and to that extent it is responsible for a great deal more misery in human hearts than ought to be necessary.

Marriage is more than romance, however much that highly

desirable element adds to it. If romance fades, however, there needs to be something firmer on which to base that marriage or it will fall. The extent to which we rely on romance is known to many a pastor who has counseled the distraught victim of infidelity. Such a one so often says, " I don't want to hold him any more if he doesn't love me," and thereby finis is written for another marriage. The supposition that erotic love and romance comprise the basis for marriage can be rationalized to allow for a new romantic attachment, and another marriage, when the same feeling is experienced again.

Seldom has the thinness of romantic marriage been better expressed than in Sloan Wilson's *The Man in the Gray Flannel Suit*. Tom has a lovely wife, Betsy, but during combat duty in Italy he develops a romantic attachment for Maria, who becomes his mistress, and after the war he begins to devote his life to a new love of monetary success. In the climax of the novel, Betsy confronts her husband with:

" Let's be honest about it. We haven't had much of a life together. You and I seem to have learned a lot since the war — a lot of things I don't want to know. We've learned to drag along from day to day without any real emotion except worry. We've learned to make love without passion. We've even learned to stop fighting together, haven't we? We haven't had a good fight since you threw that vase against the wall a year ago. We used to fight a lot when we were first married, but we don't really care enough to fight any more, do we? I haven't even cried for months. I think I've forgotten how to cry. All I know how to do nowadays is be responsible and dutiful and deliberately cheerful for the sake of the children. And all you know how to do is work day and night and worry. You give a good sermon on love, but I haven't seen much of it around here. It's a great life, isn't it? " (p. 294).

Whoever holds her mate only by the tenuous thread of romantic love is ever plagued by the possibility that he will find a younger and more freshly romantic attachment to cling to instead. How often the cult of romance has used just such an excuse to destroy a marriage could hardly be computed. But it is almost logical — if we marry for love and love alone, why should we not shed that marriage when a newer and more thrilling love passes our way? Sören Kierkegaard's *Works of Love* (tr. by David F. and Lillian M. Swenson) has the answer to such sophistry: "The task does not consist in finding the lovable object; but the task consists in finding the object already given or chosen — lovable, and in continuing to find him lovable however changed he is" (page 129). Kierkegaard indeed is suggesting something far different, something nearer the steadfast love that the Bible knows. This kind does not "alter when it alteration finds" because its roots reach deep below the romantic illusion. This kind loves in spite of the sometimes unlovable nature of the spouse, in spite of the disappointments and broken hopes encountered in marriage, in spite of in-laws, mortgages, and sick children. For contradictions, misunderstandings, and competition also are part of matrimonial relationships, and Otto Piper is right when he claims in *The Christian Interpretation of Sex* that the divinely founded unity comes to unbroken expression in rare moments only.

It is the unitive relationship that reaches deeper than romantic attachment and makes marriage Christian. Martin Buber sees the unitive dimension of marriage as revealing the Thou of two people to one another: "Out of this a marriage is built up by the Thou that is neither of the I's. This is the metaphysical and metapsychical factor of love, to which feelings of love are mere accompaniments" (*I and Thou,* p. 46). Here flows a deeper stream that reveals a divine relationship that makes all the difference in the world. Hear Buber again: "He who loves a woman, and brings her life to present realization in his, is able to look in the Thou of her eyes into a beam of the eternal Thou." God is present in that unitive bond. This God himself established, and made the sexes complementary to each other.

It has been noted that so often those three little words "I love you" might only mean "I love me, and want you for myself." When that is the meaning, the romantic protestation does not consider the other to be a Thou at all, but a mere It, a possession, a toy. But in God's creation marriage is clearly meant to be community. It is here that we learn to live not as individuals but as persons bound up together, in a continuum of life in community, from generation to generation.

Marriage Is a Covenant

There is a note of grimness in every wedding service. It is recognized frankly that marriage has a worse side: sickness, financial problems, temptations. The promises exacted on this occasion demand faithfulness through hard seasons as well as through better times of health, wealth, and fidelity. Since marriage encounters tragedy as well as bluebirds of happiness, a marriage of stability must be wrought out of something firmer than romantic love. In Christian marriage this element is the recognition that it takes three to make a marriage: a man, a woman, and God. It is his presence that hallows it, offering whatever permanence it is to have.

When two people therefore take their vows, the promises are made not only to one another but also *before God*. Paul Ramsey, in a series in *Crossroads* magazine entitled " God and the Family " (July, 1955) made clear that marriage is a covenant and that we cannot understand the importance of fidelity in matrimony until we know what covenant means in the history of Israel and the Christian Church. " Thou shalt not commit adultery " has implication of covenant fidelity; and the Bible offers many examples of analogy between forsaking one's religion and forsaking one's marriage. In Biblical language, the Hebrew word *hesed* implies complete fidelity to those with whom a covenant is made. *Hesed* gathers up a group of other and secondary meanings severally translated as mercy, loving-kindness, and steadfast love, as in, " The Lord is slow to anger and plenteous in *hesed*." The term is in frequent use in Old Testament passages, involving God's rule of covenant.

Now Christian marriage is far more than a civil contract or a social institution. It is also a covenant. According to the popular service in *The Book of Common Worship* the bride and groom " do promise and covenant before God and these witnesses " to be loving and faithful. For this covenant relation as for every other, the blessing of God is invoked. And the quality of *hesed,* that is steadfast love in complete fidelity, is essential. The archetype of marriage, as Karl Barth shows, is neither in sociology nor in nature, but in the relation of God to his people Israel.

Still another Hebrew word illuminates the Christian marriage relationship. That word is *yada'*, or "know." It will be remembered that Adam *knew* Eve and that she bore his children. This selfsame term is used to tell how God cares for his people: "O Lord, thou hast searched me and *known* me" (Ps. 139:1) or "For he *knoweth* our frame; he remembereth that we are dust" (Ps. 103:14). Obviously the verb *yada'* does not confine its meaning to sexual intercourse. True it is that a man and woman know each other in mutuality this way, and they discover much about their own manhood and womanhood by this means. However, we get no clue to the use of *yada'* in the psalm selections above unless we understand that this kind of knowledge also involves *belonging* in covenant.

This idea seems to have been caught by Richard Aldrich in his biographical tribute to his actress wife, Gertrude Lawrence. About her he wrote: "As an actress, Gertrude Lawrence is a beloved figure to millions. Bewitching and elusive as a moonbeam, she flitted from the terrace of the Carleton at Cannes to a millionaire's yacht off Palm Beach, enchanting her audiences, rekindling in their hearts something which in too many of us dims and flickers out after first youth. But Mrs. A. is a woman who was known slightly to not more than a dozen persons. And fully, intimately to only one — myself." (*Gertrude Lawrence as Mrs. A.*, pp. 3, 4.)

The covenant concept of marriage relationship is then lifted to a higher plane than romantic love ever dreamed, even in the most glowing songs of troubadours or the most romantic of motion pictures. It is put on a level where those who have a higher commitment in religious faith will better comprehend the meaning of their marriage. Far more significant than romantic love, covenant marriage is capable of bridging the depths of despair that wreck so many couples. It looks to a higher power far beyond the partner, making it possible for each to give to the other the love and understanding that is needed. Such a commitment makes us able to accept each other even when he or she is unacceptable because it draws upon a strength held in reserve.

Sex and Personality Are One

Dr. Kinsey's data have been misleading. They tend to consider sexual behavior apart from the whole personality of the individual. Sexual experience is not isolated from the rest of our being. We are bound up in one bundle of desire, guilt, fear, concern, anxieties, or whatever. And the desire we feel is not confined to genital organs, nor is it the sexual response alone that we seek in another. Normally it is the complete person sexually attracted to seek meaning and community with another complete person.

Sex expresses many other emotions than the erotic. It can be the expression of lust for power in a man, the need for acceptance by a lonely and promiscuous girl, even revenge in a marital partner. Sexual problems encountered in a sick marriage are seldom treated by the pastor-counselor in themselves; instead he looks for indications of underlying difficulty in attitudes, home conditions, and emotional maturity. Our sexual capacity does not determine the kind of persons we are, but the kind of persons we are determines our sexual expression. Success in sexual technique does not necessarily save a failing marriage; and sexual failure seldom kills a strong one. A person's sex is his most conspicuous attribute (we may not remember faces or names, residences, or opinions, but we never forget whether a person was a man or a woman). Each of us is a psychosexual being whose ways of thinking and moving are influenced by masculinity or femininity. We are what we are because of manhood or womanhood; our glands and their secretions are sex-determined. This basic sexual orientation far outweighs the influence of the coital act. Our response is as man or woman, for that is how we were created from the beginning.

One Flesh

Early in the Bible, actually in the second chapter of Genesis, occurs a term that is repeated over and again. That term is " one flesh." It designates the sexual connection of man and wife, but it infers something deeper than mere physical intercourse. The bold inference is that God is in this act; and by this means his creativity is carried forth. Derrick S. Bailey, author of *The Mystery of Love and Marriage,* has written a veritable Biblical theology of sexual intercourse by tracing this one-flesh concept (in the Greek, *henosis*) through the Scriptures. Husband and wife are one in marriage, according to this author, because *henosis* gives to their family life a certain metaphysical unity. This dimension of marriage involves a vocation of such integrity and vitality that it can be shared with the children, and can permeate an entire family with its spirit.

Derrick Bailey sees the activity of God in the coital act, blessing it or judging it, for he writes: " Sexual intercourse is an act of the whole self which affects the whole self; it is a personal encounter between man and woman in which each does something to the other, for good or for ill, which can never be obliterated. This remains true even when they are ignorant of the radical character of their act. It cannot, therefore, be treated simply as sensual indulgence. Fornication is more than an isolated, pleasurable exercise of the sexual organs; it is the expression of an attitude of mind in which God, other persons, and the self are all involved " (p. 53). Thus utilizing a power we barely understand, we encounter God where he was unexpected!

Carefully he distinguishes between *henosis* and *eros*. In *henosis* man and wife grow ever together in a deep satisfaction and faithfulness; this is a sex act that involves consent also for the numerous consequences and ramifications that result from it. In *eros* they desire the beloved in a selfish way, to have and to hold. One flesh, on the other hand, is a union of the whole man and the whole woman at the deepest level. In it they are something new and different from the persons they are when alone.

When a man and a woman are united in love through *henosis,* there must be complete fidelity to guarantee its permanence. This is a fidelity not simply to each other but to God who blessed them in this relationship. In this view, fidelity is not " required only of those who have consummated their love and who have become 'one flesh.' It is demanded from all lovers from the very moment they accept their vocation and know that thenceforth their lives are bound together in a single destiny" (*The Mystery of Love and Marriage*, p. 21).

Something of this same concept of one-flesh unity is felt by many a married couple who have never thought of it in this wise. With an inkling that God has enriched their love relationship in the tenderness of one-flesh relationship, they have sometimes been surprised by an awareness of God's nearness and they have caught glimpses of a deeper emotion and understanding than they had ever known. Their human love (*eros*), which encompasses the sexual relationship, can be transformed by the blessing of godlike love (*agape*); and the two become commingled in a mystery that is older than time. While such a theory flies in the face of the tremendous teaching of Anders Nygren in *Agape and Eros*, I feel that his too-incisive dissection of these two forms of love has robbed marriage of some of its central meaning. Although Nygren would cleave *agape* from *eros*, pitting these two against each other and placing *eros* in an unredeemable status, the theory can be stoutly defended that our self-seeking love (*eros*) can be gloriously altered by the introduction of the accepting, nonhostile characteristics of divine love (*agape*).

Sexual love in marriage then is something holy and to be treated with due reverence. It was this conviction that led William Temple to say that he " would no more joke about sex than he would joke about Holy Communion — and for exactly the same reason. To joke about it is to treat with lightness something that deserves reverence." (*Christian Faith and Life*, p. 49.) Moreover, there comes into the relationship of one flesh a new altruism because in this act the individual discovers who he is in the revelation of another and beloved person. Now he is enabled to mature in a new way wherein he sees his spouse as a Thou and not as a mere sexual object (as an it). She is no means to an end; but she is a partner in a deep and holy love where God is also present. In the brilliant insight of Reuel L. Howe, this means that the sexual act of a Christian couple can be a means of salvation. Here can be found the union of flesh and spirit, of human love and divine love. By its light they can accept their family, their problems, and their vocation.

When God gave to man and woman this power and this relationship, he put into their bodies the ability to create for him. This we call procreation. But that which is procreated is not only progeny; it is also love and faith, maturity and strength. What is more, the Christian act of procreation includes God, and this act cannot ever be considered apart from him and his grace.

The Pastor in Marriage Counseling

Because of improved health conditions and the lengthening life span, people marrying today can look forward to a longer lifetime together than ever before — if their marriage remains in repair. Happy marriage is not a happenstance along the road to romance. It is built slowly and lovingly by two maturing people who want to find security and acceptance in each other and in their children. No easy task, this kind of married life needs patience, time, and occasionally repair work. " Marriage is an art, but many people are conducting it as though it were a sort of unskilled labor," writes Leland Foster Wood. " Instead of learning the art of marriage at its best, they go along as bunglers making a sorry picture of what oftentimes might be the finest sort of marriage. . . . Instead of contributing their best to their home life they sometimes contribute their worst and bring out the worst in each other." (*How Love Grows in Marriage,* p. 67.)

The most common danger to marriage is a failure of communication. T. S. Eliot has characterized these broken relationships with devastating simplicity in *The Cocktail Party* (pp. 139, 140) :

> " They do not repine;
> Are contented with the morning that separates
> And with the evening that brings together
> For casual talks before the fire
> Two people who know they do not understand each other,
> Breeding children whom they do not understand
> And who will never understand them."

That the clergyman has an immense advantage in marriage counseling is readily seen in his work. Often he has performed the marriage ceremony, and he has an interest in making that marriage succeed. He lives close to his people and he knows something of their ways and of their problems. If he does a workmanlike job in the premarital counseling, he has access into their family for postmarital counseling too. He has a continuing relationship and can request that when crises occur (the recognition that they will occur is therapeutic in itself), they might come to him instead of going to friends, relatives, or the law, for he is just as interested in keeping them married as he was in getting them married.

But the pastor also knows that marriage counseling is a difficult, intricate job. It touches the deepest emotions of life, and becomes mixed with a most complicated network of relationships. Often it is an entirely thankless service, with large risks of failure and of pain. If we stumble in the attempt, we may increase the disturbance in already disturbed people, and take severe risks with their opportunities for a solution to their problems. The pastor, moreover, must overcome some obstacles in himself to marital counseling; sometimes he is timid, or concerned about his own marital situation, hesitant about his skill or his training. Larger obstacles quite beyond his control can cut his usefulness in counseling considerably. Accidents and disaster can play havoc with the lives of church families. Yet with faith in God and with careful work, life can be rebuilt and marriages can be reconciled.

In time the observant pastor learns to recognize the distress signals in marriage relations: nasty joking, sudden spirited clashes, loss of common interests, breakdown of communication with each other, utter apathy or constant absences from the home. Marriage problems frequently are caused by the same factors that cause failures in other realms of life: personality problems, immaturity, anxieties. If one or both of the persons is neurotic, then these factors may be compounded in seriousness, and are unlikely to have been solved by marriage. The outside chance that marriage itself can somehow help people to overcome their personality defects has spurred many people into matrimony who reconsider this vain hope at leisure.

If the pastor in his round of calls senses that some of these conditions exist, he may come upon a sick marriage before it is beyond remedy. He can see the signs of resentment, chronic irritability, the decrease in affection, the indications of restlessness, of boredom, and of dissatisfaction. He may walk in on a developing crisis in time to lead his people to talk to him about their feelings and their concerns, and this is an advantage. Generally the earlier a marital conflict is treated, the more favorable the prognosis.

The pastor has limitations as a marriage counselor, but he also has a great strength, for he is part of an enduring community in which the love of God is related to the needs of his children. That pastors should ever neglect their spiritual resources is a scandal of the ministry. Knowing that the power of Christ can help people master their problems, and help them live at a higher level than some shabby second-best, the pastor to his shame still attempts sometimes to guide people to solutions that take no account of their faith. Canon T. Guy Rogers, an Englishman, puts it straight: " No one on behalf of the Church ought to be allowed to handle the disagreements of married people who does not believe quite fervently in the power of conversion and the immediate influence of Christ on the lives of the people of today " (Canon T. Guy Rogers in a book *The Church and the People,* quoted by Leslie Weatherhead in *The Mastery of Sex Through Psychology and Religion,* p. 166).

A touching scene is re-created by Rev. Margaret Blair Johnstone in her *Create Your Own Tomorrow* (p. 238), in which she tells of how the knowledge of the love and power of God had a healing effect:

" ' There is no use in going in there,' a despairing husband once said. ' Jennie is in another coma. There is nothing anyone can do.'

" ' Perhaps not,' I admitted, ' but then again, perhaps there is. At any rate, I would like to go in and I would like you to come with me.'

"Together Jim and I went into Jennie's room. Completely motionless she lay. Taking Jim's hand, I placed it on Jennie's. 'Years ago,' I said, 'you two promised that for better, for worse, for richer, for poorer, in sickness and in health, you would love and cherish each other. That promise has brought you through many a trial. It can bring you through this trial. Let us pray to God that it will.'

"Weeks later Jennie stopped in to see me. 'I couldn't move,' she told me. 'There was no way I could let you and Jim know. But when I heard those blessed words I made up my mind that this time too it would be for better, not worse. I vowed with all that was in me to fight with all I had to make your prayer come true.'"

Methods of Marriage Counseling

"It is one thing to tell people that a marriage relationship should be founded in an attitude of mutuality and co-operation," Carroll A. Wise reminds us; "it is quite another thing to help a person work through self-centered attitudes and come to the place where he can enter into a mutual and co-operative relationship" (*Pastoral Counseling; Its Theory and Practice*, p. 186). How true this is becomes known quickly to the counselor who seeks to bring some healing touch to a sick marriage. Stepping warily lest he disrupt it more, the pastor regards marriage counseling as one of his toughest assignments. Even the upset marriage may have more love in it than at first is apparent. This is no place for a lecture, or a list of resolutions, nor even to deal with what we dub common sense. His direct task is to ease a change in feelings and attitudes so that their entire relationship can be changed. Otherwise their underlying troubles in relationship can crop out again in still other issues.

If both man and wife come for counseling, the counselor has reason to hope for some success because tacitly they have already accepted responsibility for the outcome. Then both marriage partners will move together in their insights and understanding, even though they are seen independently. If only one of them agrees to counseling, some gains can still be made at least in a supportive way. A permissive, encouraging counselor can help ease the burden. It is possible that the one who comes alone can later bring the spouse. It is advisable for the pastor to watch his language at this point. Sometimes we ask to meet the other partner so as to learn another *side* of the story; and in that one word we indicate an adversary as in competitive sports rivalry. It is preferable to infer that we see some of the picture now, and would like to see it also from another *view*. This term is not so loaded.

An interesting technique of encouraging some mutuality was practiced by the late Fritz Künkel, who used to see each partner independently and confidentially to let them express their situation. Then he would send them a joint letter summing up his impressions (apart from the confidences). This pulled it all together at an early stage and clarified what might be expected in further interviews. At the outset it is well to caution them to remain silent about the counseling. The fewer people they talk to, the better for the counselor, for if he is the only one with whom they discuss this relationship, he can be of more aid in a less confused situation.

By the second interview, the counselor might draw out from each person his feelings about having married in the first place. Was it for romance, for money, or perhaps for status? The client may not be able to tell; or he may not recognize the true reasons himself (perhaps it appeared to be romance, but it was a satisfaction of certain dependency needs). To isolate the factors that led to marriage will aid in learning why and how it has come to be a disappointment. It must be acknowledged that a vaguely disturbed couple may not understand the source of their difficulty. They often mention some factor, e.g., sex problems or money squabbles, but they seldom recognize when they have been turning their own resentments toward a marriage partner. It should surprise no pastor to learn that the problem sometimes lies in the very one who brings the complaint, his or her unreasonable demands upon the other being only a projection of some inner anxiety. The counselor's cue is to work on these resentments; then the obstacle may be cleared away sufficiently for the couple themselves to solve the nagging problems of their everyday living. Although the pastor is powerless to help one who resists help, he can draw out resentful feelings of a frustrated parishioner and lead toward new insights about marriage.

Such insights may be far from the pastor's conception of ideal marriage, but his work is not to remake other marriages into models of his own. What comprises a livable relationship for one couple may not for another. This is their problem, and sympathetic though he is, the pastor ever remains outside in a spirit of interest, yet of detachment.

As he does not force his solution upon the couple, neither does he force his religious ideas. Faith has a healing effect upon these relationships only so far as the people are able to understand and act on their basic Christian attitudes. However, when they are mature enough to depend upon their Christian faith for support in the reorganization of their living or in the process of forgiving one another, there is no therapy to match it.

Many pastors use some mechanical device such as a check list to guide their search for background and undercurrents of the marital rift. Among the customary topics that evoke some response are attitudes toward money, in-laws, premarital experiences, vocation, fears, guilt, religious faith, quarrels and making up, parenthood and children, health conditions, childhood memories, home conditions, and avocations. Each counselor tends to concentrate on his own set of most useful topics. Always, however, he is listening for that feeling tone that reveals basic attitudes and degrees of self-acceptance. If the person cannot stand himself because of guilt, inferiority, or some neurosis, he will be unable to accept his spouse, family, job — or counselor. When love has been unfulfilled through years of life, it will not be corrected in mere minutes of counseling. A person can only live with others who can live with himself. And learning to abide oneself is a lifelong struggle, involving not only our marriage relationships but the entire family, not only human contacts but also our peace with God and acceptance of his ever-waiting forgiveness. The pastoral counselor who is mindful of these factors will bring a healing touch to the sick marriage.

Infidelity Tests the Counselor

Because it is dramatic, and yet old as time itself, the marriage relationship broken by infidelity is perhaps the most challenging that the counselor faces. An arresting case history recorded by Sylvanus M. Duvall in *Men, Women and Morals* (pp. 283–284) presents the issue without detour:

"Hazel Church and Bob Skipper were obviously in love with each other. You could tell it by the way Bob helped Hazel remove her coat in the office of the marriage counselor. It was evident in the way their hands touched each other as they sat side by side. The adoring glances which they turned toward each other constantly telegraphed their message of love. They made you feel like putting your hands on their heads in benediction and wishing them Godspeed. There was just one catch in it. Bob was already married to another. They had one child, and a second on the way.

"Their story made you feel even more concerned. Bob had recently been discharged from the Navy. While in the service he had been stationed in a city on the West Coast. There he had met Hazel. They had met in a church where Hazel worked as a member of the staff. Their common interest in religion was one of the factors which drew them together. They began to 'date,' quite innocently at first, and quickly 'fell in love' with each other. In the meantime, Bob's wife had been living in Cleveland with her mother and a four-year-old son. This arrangement seemed more satisfactory than having her come to a city in which accommodations were so limited. With his wife thus safely out of the way, Bob moved in with Hazel and lived with her for three months. The wife was, of course, not informed.

"But Mrs. Skipper became lonesome for her husband. She informed Bob that she and their son were coming west, and Bob was able to locate a fairly suitable apartment. When she arrived, Bob introduced her to Hazel. The wife, suspecting nothing, welcomed Hazel into the family circle and invited her on their trips and outings. Bob continued to consort with Hazel, dividing his nights between the two women. He explained his absences from his wife as naval duties. The wife, still deeply in love with her husband, had no inkling of the situation. The illicit lovers finally decided that the husband should become divorced and they would then marry each other. They came for consultation as to how best to proceed."

Confronted by a case of adultery, the Christian counselor must take care that he spend less time on the nature of the sexual sin and more on its underlying conditions. For until we learn that sex attitudes are rooted deep in the personality structure, we will deal on the surface with moralisms and scandal, and these are notoriously useless as counseling aids. When we discover that infidelity is part of the marital problem, we may be sure that we are dealing with suffering persons, often burdened by a heavy guilt. They can project their guilt upon other causes — the nagging spouse, age differences in marriage, incompatibility, lovelessness, loneliness, sex dissatisfactions in marriage, *et alii*. These, to be sure, complicate the problem; but the person who continues to cheat at sex is immature and in need of growing up.

Though Alfred Kinsey verified through his samplings of the American population that adultery is not uncommon, society still conditions us to respond strongly to any kind of sexual dishonesty. The tabloid newspapers, the town gossip, the harshness of the community all evidence this strong reaction, often punishing severely the persons who had been led to expect an easy tolerance. The age-old desire for sex variety has no place in the building of satisfactory marriage, a process that requires both love and discipline. Even the marriage that has a high degree of sexual frustration is not improved by sexual explorations outside. This complicating tendency creates more problems than it solves. Reconciliation becomes almost impossible in some cases where pride is injured and trust is broken — but not solely because of the sexual athlete's offenses. The unforgiving nature of an unbending spouse may be as much the counselor's concern as the philanderer's wanderings.

Dissatisfaction with a marriage presents an excuse for infidelity only to the immature person who is unwilling to work at the job of improving his marriage. When the adjustment is difficult, this is no reason to begin again with a new partner in some clandestine relationship. Incompatibility is the name we seem to give to a marriage that does not yet fit. André Maurois has a mature view of it: "I have chosen. From now on my aim will be not to search for someone who may please me, but to please the one I have chosen." (In *Marriage: The Art of Lasting Love,* by David R. Mace, p. 153.)

Dealing with infidelity, then, the pastor-counselor looks to the matter of immaturity, refrains from blame and judgment (need it be said again?), and works to build anew the foundations of Christian marriage. He will find useful referrals to such biological aid as will clear up some of the sexual difficulty. (The pastor is advised to avail himself of the several leaflets for counselors that the American Institute of Family Relations, 5287 Sunset Blvd., Los Angeles, has prepared on impotence, frigidity, and the sexual adjustment in marriage.) But he will know that to solve the sex riddle alone is not enough. The marriage partners will still have to develop into mature persons, able to understand and accept their weaknesses, but able also to mobilize their strengths. For this discipline there is no substitute for a carefully constructed Christian marriage.

Divorce Confronts the Pastor

It would be easier for the Church legalists of our day if Jesus had been a legalist. His teachings on divorce and remarriage are confusing and inacceptable now to the very sort of folk to whom they were inacceptable then. It was to the literalists then that he addressed himself; it is today's literalists who misunderstand him once more. Our Lord's teaching was the gospel, not a new code of legal regulations; and the gospel is proclaimed in a spirit of love and forgiveness. Nevertheless, a dismaying quantity of Church law has been enacted and executed in an unforgiving, vengeful spirit. Nowhere is this truer than in the case of divorce and remarriage; and the pastor needs to understand the Biblical roots of the problem so that he can counsel with divorced persons and make wise Christian decisions when asked to remarry them.

It must be remembered that Jesus did not deliver his principles concerning divorce and remarriage in some setting of splendid isolation. He lived in the thick of a divorce-ridden culture. A controversy about interpretation of divorce laws was

even then raging; and his words as quoted (or are they mis-
quoted?) in the Gospels arise in reply to specific, troubled questions. Two rabbis of the time, Shammai and Hillel, were deep in
conflict about how to interpret Deut. 24:1-4, particularly that
passage which reads, " When a man hath taken a wife, and married her, and it come to pass that she find no favor in his eyes,
because he hath found some uncleanness in her: then let him
write her a bill of divorcement." The question was just what
could be considered " some uncleanness." Hillel, the liberal
rabbi, was inclined to allow a large variety of objectionable features to be subsumed under uncleanness — even poor cooking.
Shammai, on the other hand, strictly interpreted uncleanness as
unchastity and nothing else.

This rabbinical controversy is reflected in the Gospel accounts:
we trace influences of Shammai in Matthew's writing (Matt.
5:32 and 19:9), and of Hillel in the Marcan version (Mark 10:11,
12) and the Lucan account (Luke 16:18). It is Matthew only who
writes: " Who divorces his wife, *except on the ground of unchastity . . .*" The others omit this phrase. New Testament
scholars have come to believe that " except on the ground of unchastity " is a gloss inserted by the Jewish community at Antioch
ca. A.D. 80 in order to bring an interpretation of the words of
Jesus closer to the Mosaic legal code. However, Paul, the apostle
to Gentiles, lined himself with the Mark-Luke interpretation
and wrote in a letter to the churchmen at Corinth: " If the un-
believing partner desires to separate, let it be so; in such a case
the brother or sister is not bound. For God has called us to peace."
(I Cor. 7:15.)

In recent years Protestant Churches have entered a period of
agonizing reappraisal concerning the Biblical words of divorce.
Since these four New Testament quotations are not easily reconciled, different Churches have permitted differing interpretations.
We know that neither Jesus nor Paul favored a relentless legal-
ism that binds a disciple in every conceivable circumstance. The
Matthaean and Lucan accounts, moreover, show that Jesus was
answering a difficult question put to him by a critical group of
Pharisees. Under these circumstances there may be justifiable rea-

son to interpret his statements as a stern reply to a not altogether sincere question phrased by men who sought to trap him. If this is so, it is unrealistic to quote any of these several versions as an inflexible rule for all people, henceforth and forever. We do not argue that Jesus was legislating absolute law when he said, " Lay not up for yourselves treasures upon earth," or, " Swear not at all."

Ever one to plunge beneath the superficial tensions to ultimate causes, Jesus emphasized God's creation of man and woman to become one flesh in marriage, and added: " Whom therefore God hath joined together, let no man put asunder." Thus did he nail his teaching in the eternal will of God for his people. The modern pastor who finds himself confronted by the practical aspects of this issue in the broken marriages of parishioners is advised to recall something of the intention of Jesus in his gospel of love. His statements must be seen not as separate, disconnected items but as an inseparable portion of that gospel, based on forgiveness, pardon, and new opportunity to redeem past failures through the grace of God. Thus even marital failure for causes other than adultery is not beyond forgiveness. It is odd that the Church must occasionally be reminded in this connection, as well as in others, of its gospel of forgiveness for the repentant sinner. Recollection of Jesus' forgiveness in the *cause célèbre* of the adulterous woman (John 8:1-11) reveals his attitude toward one who dramatically transgressed the marriage vow. Even in this disputed passage, the intention of Jesus is clear: it holds the whole person in deep respect and forgives much. As Dean Inge summed up the matter in his book *Christian Ethics and Modern Problems* (pp. 388, 390): " In all our Lord's words about marriage it is not the occasional wreckage of a union which is in his mind, but the institution as God means it to be — the sacrament of love, which must be kept in ' sanctification and honor.' . . . My conclusion is that Christ meant to inculcate a higher view of the sacredness of marriage than had been held by the rabbis of either school. I do not think he meant to lay down hard and fast rules. If a very hard case had been brought before him, he might possibly have said, as he said about another commandment, ' marriage was made for man, not man for marriage.' "

While much of the Church was trying to make a law out of the Matthaean account of Jesus' teachings, and sometimes inferring that the exception "for adultery" composed a *duty* to divorce instead of a *permit* to divorce, Church members still sought divorce to discontinue their marriages for other reasons as well. Relentless and sadistic cruelty has broken up marriages also; moral degeneration has led to divorce courts; immaturity has been at the bottom of countless separations. These, in fact, may have been the real problems in a marriage where adultery, resultantly cropped up. Some denominations, recognizing this, allow other causes in their Church law, or leave the interpretation of the matter to pastors.

All this discussion of standards and law glosses over the essential personal factor. Divorce seldom hits a clergyman directly, but to his people it can be the realest experience of life. Wayne E. Oates in his book *Anxiety in Christian Experience* brilliantly traces that the loss occasioned by separation and divorce parallels the course of grief that follows death of a loved one. This is precisely why the pastor must counsel with the divorced person, in a supportive relationship with him or her. Only empathic pastors have any inkling as to its pain, and those who fail to realize the nature of such grief are capable of compounding the problem. God certainly must be more merciful than some of his ministers and theologians can be when they slip into legalisms. In a letter to *The Christian Century* sometime ago, one woman wrote: " In the sudden alarm over increasing divorces, I wonder if ministers realize how they are offending divorcees in the pews. I come from a deeply religious family. I have taught young people in church schools and worked in churches all my life. My husband, a minister, left me when our children were babies. Now Sunday after Sunday I am told about the sin of divorce. . . . I am employed in a law office and know that divorce is perfectly legal; yet [my] church calls it a sin. Last Sunday the head of the missionary department of one of our large denominations preached that no Christian home could be built on divorce. I challenge that statement. My children, now grown, are religious and in church work and will agree that our home has maintained a spiritual emphasis. Isn't there a better way of combating divorce than by maligning the innocent victims? " (July 10, 1946, p. 872.)

Divorce and remarriage remain repugnant to the Church because they testify to a failure of the one-flesh relationship that might have built a Christian home. Yet, as Karl Barth suggests, this may be the better way in which two people " can be restored to new obedience " (*Karl Barth's Church Dogmatics,* by Otto Weber, tr. by Arthur C. Cochrane, p. 221).

So long have we been working through the agonizing problems of divorce that some sociologists consider Protestantism actually to be a contributory cause to divorce. But we are not alone. Roman Catholicism also has its divorce allowable within canon law, as when a practicing Catholic is prohibited from his religious obligations by a marital partner who is not in sympathy with, say, parochial schooling or attendence at Mass. More frequent, but not easy, is annulment, which is a declaration in a Church court that a marriage never existed; Thomistic tradition allows nine causes for which annulment is justifiable. For centuries Roman Catholics took advantage of fictitious evidence of clandestinism (a marriage that had been secretly and unofficially joined) — just as some people today set up fictitious evidence of adultery to obtain a divorce. Social researchers have lately ascertained in several samplings that the most frequent kind of marital breakup in Roman Catholic families is simple separation without benefit of clergy or court.

The Divorce Rate

Much nonsense has been written about divorce statistics, most of which tends to give a less accurate and less encouraging picture than facts warrant. The marriage-divorce ratio expresses the number of marriages in any given year in relation to the number of divorces in the same year. In the 1950's this ratio hovered around four marriages to one divorce. This does not mean that one in every four marriages is going to end in divorce; and such a use of statistics, however well it is meant, is careless. More accurately, this ratio is used as an index of the net change in our married population in any given year, i.e., four families were added to the married population for every one lost in divorce. The divorce rate refers to the number of divorces in a given year per 1,000 population at the beginning of the same year. Some 29 states keep vital statistics on marriage and divorce, but there is not enough uniformity in this standard across the nation to give an accurate divorce rate for the U.S.A. A careful guesstimate puts it at 2.5 divorces per 1,000 at the time of the 1950 census.

What is behind it all? Excessive drinking, infidelity, in-law strife, loss of romance, poor housing, sexual maladjustment, religious differences, and financial difficulties are all given as reasons for marital failure. Underneath many of these reasons often lie emotional immaturity, personality defects, ignorance, or a breakdown in communication. Sad to relate, divorce decrees are awarded daily to couples who need instead to have some repair work done on personality. The best time to avoid divorce is before marriage. If then the counseling and selective process is wise, a groundwork can be built that makes split-ups less likely. It has been wisely said that the pastor who does no premarital educating has no right to preach against divorce. But it would not be enough for him to deplore their plight anyway. Actually there are greater evils than divorce. Sometimes great harm can be done in keeping a family together. We ought to avoid the pitfall of supposing that by merely keeping a home intact we are doing *ipso facto* a Christian act. A reconciliation could conceivably prolong and complicate a situation of cruelty or one where a marriage is already dead. Yet the clergyman will always be alert to possibilities of mending broken relationships and helping families to re-establish their stability.

In a case where nothing more can be done for the marriage, the pastor still has a responsibility to work with the divorced persons, to help each one find himself or herself through faith, to assist in that re-evaluation of life which looks steadily toward the future with courage, to orient such persons in the church fellowship with prayer and care so that they are not left alone. Now, if ever, a person needs to hear the glad tidings of God's good news. This is no time (there never is any) to cast aside the divorce and to condemn divorce at all costs. With Emil Brunner, in *The Divine Imperative* (p. 362), the pastor will see divorce not as an evil that requires reproof but as a weakness that cries for strength:

" Between the maintenance of the idea of marriage as an unbreakable relation of fidelity and the command to love one's neighbor as oneself, God's Command must here be perceived in a spirit of free decision, and obedience must be achieved. Here, above all, the judgment of the Christian believer must shake off all the trammels of civil law: above all, it must free itself from the prejudice which is based upon the confusion of thought to which we have already alluded — the view that implies that the maintenance of marriage under all circumstances is what God requires, and that divorce is forbidden by him, so that divorce can only be considered at all as a concession to weakness. Certainly the fact of a divorce is a sign of weakness, and is a specially clear indication that we are an ' adulterous generation.' But cases are possible where not to divorce might be a sign of greater weakness, and might be a still greater offense against the Divine order."

Whether the late Alfred C. Kinsey was correct or not in his assertion that " there may be nothing more important in a marriage than a determination that it shall persist " (*Sexual Behavior in the Human Female,* Vol. II, p. 11), it does seem obvious that many homes are broken that are not compelled to be, that many divorcees are worse off after marriage than before; and they know it. When the Church gets its head out of the sand, is willing to admit that divorce does exist, and may even be justifiable in some instances, it will better be able to help people with problems and save more homes.

There are no less than forty-nine different divorce laws in the U.S.A. (the District of Columbia grants divorce too) because the Constitution left this prerogative to the states. Migratory divorce, the result of moving to that state with the lowest requirements for legal residence, has made a mockery of tighter legislation. Yet it is doubtful whether a national uniform divorce law or stricter requirements would work much reform. State laws already resemble each other closely, and the semi-bootleg nature of this abuse (as in the days of liquor prohibition) is less the result of poor enforcement than it is the attitude of society. To stem the tide of divorce, we need first to work with its primary cause — marriage.

Divorce proves to be a disillusioning experience for many reasons, and not the least of these is the attitude of the law. Unfortunately divorce procedure proceeds along lines of "adversary litigation" in order to arrive at the "truth" by naming one person as "guilty" and the other "innocent." There is a plaintiff and a defendant. Evidence must be introduced that proves the law is fulfilled in providing grounds for divorce. In practice, most couples choose the most innocuous category they can find, and this usually turns out to be some form of cruelty. But in this case, cruelty can mean almost anything in the wide gamut between assault and insult. The plaintiff and the defendant in a divorce suit are often prevented by their lawyers from speaking to one another, or from showing any signs that might be interpreted as reconciliation lest the divorce action between them be slowed. In order to work the divorce within the laws of the state, evidence is often prearranged, perjury encouraged, testimony manufactured. Legal divorce has become what Thurman Arnold calls "a *sub rosa* institution, full of inconsistencies and insincerity." New York, for instance, allows several grounds for annulment but only one for divorce — adultery. The scandalous result: trumped-up hotel room evidence of infidelity. One disgusted judge, hearing the old evidence that a litigant was discovered in a hotel room with a woman, growled, "Maybe they met together to pray." The combined wrath of church and society has come down upon this antiquated and cumbersome system that is often anything but justice.

Divorcees Anonymous

One organization is so convinced that divorce cannot be relied upon as the solution to marital problems that it has formed an active organization known as Divorcees Anonymous. Taking a page out of the book of Alcoholics Anonymous, they also have twelve steps toward recovery, require anonymity in their publicity, and seek by means of a mutual therapy to help one another. Some of their finest work in the various cities where chapters are located is in rehabilitating those who have had recourse to divorce and in helping them to adjust to their new estate. Their meetings amount to group counseling by those who have suffered through some of the grief of divorce. Five basic attitudes are listed as a type of creed for active members:

1. Divorce is not a solution.
2. Marriage is a holy and desirable estate.
3. Development of future generations of physically, mentally, and emotionally sound persons depends upon the health and soundness of marriage and the family.
4. There is a spiritual power greater than man whose help is essential.
5. A willingness is needed to help others to a deeper understanding of, and better adjustment to, the married life.

The address of the national headquarters of Divorcees Anonymous is Box 5313, Chicago, Illinois. Urban churches with a sizable percentage of divorced and widowed people in their membership and constituency have formed organizations for social fellowship that reach these people. So often the conventionally organized groups within the church make these lonely folk feel even lonelier. Divorcees, widows, widowers, and single people feel keenly that the active family program of many parishes leaves them out. A program for such members has been amazingly successful in one Portland church where a group of some 150 men and women have semimonthly meetings for education and fellowship. While it is odd that the Church, a redemptive fellowship, has sometimes forgotten to minister to this segment of the bereft congregation, it grows increasingly difficult to forget a group who have become more numerous in our society, and whose need is so much more apparent.

7

THREE SPECIAL PROBLEMS
IN PASTORAL CARE

*" There is a more continuous opportunity for
an effective Christian ministry in the home
than anywhere else in the world. . . . In
a home . . . the ministry of word and deed
is in the closest contact with the practical
problems. . . . Accordingly such ministry,
even though the congregation is tiny, is in
close touch with reality."* — Elton Trueblood.

Of all the " helping professions," the clergy seem to receive the
widest variety of requests for assistance. Families in the parish,
and out of it, appeal to the pastor for all possible kinds of aid;
and, be it said to his credit, he makes every effort to care for
their needs. He must keep informed about a great many family
problems, and some of these (e.g., alcoholism, financial stress,
in-law conflicts) are carefully discussed in other books. However, there is need to discuss the problem of aged persons and
their family relations, the tragedy of handicapped children in
family life, and the plight of the childless. To these three topics
we now turn our attention.

I. Families and Their Aged Persons

Older persons, whose population segment has been increasing
at twice the rate of the nation's over-all growth, are in some ways
a tragic, in other ways a glorious, picture in today's world. On
the one hand it is possible to say (as a social worker did) that
penicillin removed the old man's friend when it licked pneu-

monia! On the other, it is possible to witness aged persons con-
quering new heights and making unprecedented gains.

Becoming aged in our culture so often seems to mean becoming a problem, acting crotchety, expecting attention. The senior
members of the household also find the young generations a bit
trying, and are wont to complain of the noise, the newer ways of
doing things, and the lack of respect. Where these feelings are
put together in one household, it should not be surprising that
tensions develop.

"Two thirds of older persons feel unwanted, and many of
them are right," according to Dr. Erwin Ackerknecht, of the
University of Wisconsin. They may have been retired compul-
sorily from their employment, replaced in the organizations
where they once held office, and treated as obsolete equipment
by their own families. It takes a strong personality with a clear
purpose in life to surmount the feeling of rejection that inevitably results. Many, lacking the high morale to fend off depression, lapse into sickness and recurring blues. When the oldster is
ill (and the illness can be psychosomatic under these conditions),
he may become frightened and partially disabled. That condition can also spread unhappiness throughout the family.

Some families, knowing the pitfalls of family discord in the
three-generation household, have learned ways of living together
in amity. A visitor to one home was astonished at how graciously the children of that home accepted their great-uncle's for-
getfulness and confusion, showing him affection all the while.
That kind of consideration is not learned by original thinking.
It comes about by imitation. Obviously they had seen their own
parents showing affectionate regard for the sometimes clumsy
Uncle Fred, and the youngsters supposed this to be the best way
to get along. As a matter of fact, it is.

Today's pastors find themselves increasingly embroiled in
family problems that involve older parents. Their income, their
housing, their relationships become difficult to handle, and tensions grow. In order to counsel with the aging as well as with
their families, it is good to have at hand some of the gathered experience of those who have gained skills in living with grand-

parents in the home. Usually they testify to having arrived at their methods after a series of trials and errors. Generally they cite such approaches as these:

1. Be considerate yet not patronizing of the older person. Feelings do not grow numb as we age — far from it. The aged appreciate consideration for their point of view and for their rights. But they cannot accept the superior and patronizing air of: " Now, Mother, you just sit down and rest. I'll set the table myself." This seemingly generous tone might just partly conceal the memory of spilled coffee on the tablecloth and criticism of the way Mother arranges the silver and napkins.

2. Be patient, and avoid nagging. The sight and hearing of older people often grow dim, accounting for some of their accidents as well as their failure to decide or to act quickly. Even if pressures are applied to make them react differently, such measures are apt to complicate the pattern further. Nagging can boomerang, causing the very acts it was meant to avoid.

3. Make them feel wanted and accepted. Everyone needs to feel wanted and part of the team. We are all social creatures and we get our greatest satisfactions in relationship with others; seldom are we comfortable about being dependent. Older people in the home are happier when they have duties to perform, contributions to make, advice to be sought. Here a word about honesty is advisable — if work is assigned, it has to be real, and not manufactured busywork merely for the sake of activity. The concern for their opinion has to be genuine or they will soon see through the ruse. It is genuine relationships of warmth and understanding that we all need. Robert A. Nisbet (in *The Quest for Community*) correctly lays at the door of family and social alienation the senile neuroses and psychoses of our older population.

4. Grant privacy to older people so that they still have a place to call their own. Difficult though this is for many households, it is highly important. In Nora Stirling's play *The Room Upstairs,* Fran barges into the room of her elderly mother and scolds her for doing her personal washing there. In the argument that develops many grievances spill out, and the old lady sums it up:

"How could you [understand] when you've never been old?
It's easy to understand young people because you've been one
yourself. So it's easier to make allowances for the young. But
old age — you've never been there — so you've no idea, really,
what it's like " (p. 34).

5. Be open and candid about family arrangements. It is objectionable for anyone to learn belatedly that his presence has
somehow caused plans to be altered without his realizing it, and
then to hear the martyred tone of: " Oh, it's all right. You
couldn't know how we felt about it. And we simply made the
best of it." Far better is the method of openly arriving at family
decisions even if it means frankly stating rights and plans. Fewer
feelings can be injured this way.

Family life and the attitudes of the rest of the family toward
aging are important in whether or not a person will handle his
own aging effectively. When families as a whole accept the cultural stereotypes about aging, and when parents have handled
their own aging in a negative way, any individual of that family
is much less likely to adjust well to his own aging process.

6. The aged persons do best when they make intelligent con-
cessions to the facts of aging. Knowing their limitations and adjusting to them, allowing their grown children autonomy and re-
specting them in it, trying to appreciate the opinions of others in
changed times: these attitudes go far in making a fruitful life in
later years. The Child Study Association has a Grandmothers'
Committee to help them better to understand their role. And
Dr. Dorothy V. Whipple, author of *Our American Babies,* has
suggested out of her experience this charter for grandmothers:

" Remember, your daughter is grown up and must make her own
decisions.

" Treat her as an equal and a friend, not as a child who owes you
special respect. Between adults, friendship is usually worth more than
duty.

" When the baby comes, admire him. This can hardly be overdone.

" Compliment the mother on the way she takes care of the baby.

" If you cannot do this honestly, *say nothing,* and do not even
look your disapproval.

" Remember that your experience in taking care of babies is a generation old, much has been learned about babies in this time, and *some* of the new things are good.

" Remember that the young, inexperienced mother may be, in her heart, a little afraid of your maturity and experience. She needs assurance that she is able to handle her new job. Give her that assurance by letting her know that you think the way she is doing is all right and does not need to be changed to your way.

" Help out when needed and when asked. Try to be something solid and secure that your daughter can always fall back on. You want to be useful and needed. Sometimes it may be inconvenient, but remember that a loving and loved grandmother is one of the world's great blessings."

"Then there is Grandma's side of the story, on which young parents sometimes need a bit of advice. Here it is:

" ' Share your baby with your mother.

" ' Remember that for years you have been the center of her life and work. She cannot help wanting a small share in your baby. Try to give it to her.

" ' Grandmothers have experience that young mothers lack. Do not ignore this. When there is a difference of opinion, let the doctor's advice settle the question. Sometimes you have to be very firm in your intention to bring up your baby according to present-day ideas, not ideas a generation old. Get the point across and then never harp on it.

" ' Ask for help from your mother. Usually she wants to help and will be glad to do it on your terms.

" ' Try to see the older woman's side.

" ' Be considerate.

" ' Try to build a relationship between your mother and your baby that will bring joy to both of them, and to you, too, to watch.'

" Finally, Dr. Whipple says to young mothers: ' While your baby is in your arms, start preparing to be a grand old grandma when your turn comes, as it most surely will.' "

Basic Human Relations

Now it is obvious from even a cursory reading of these points that they represent ways of dealing with people under almost any circumstances. It is a strange commentary on our mores that the courtesies of personal relationships must be spelled out when we consider the contacts between members of the same family. Social workers have noted repeatedly that the aged persons who are placed in foster boarding homes receive kinder treatment and are happier than among their own relatives whom they love. The older folks themselves must be reminded of their inconsiderate and often neglectful ways less often when they are among acquaintances than when they are in the family. In such a setting they do less criticizing, are more careful of neatness and of their dress. They expect that they shall earn respect rather than demand it. As guests in such homes, the aged are likely to indulge less in the pettiness of family intrigues, and to maintain a more independent life of their own. If they are successful in such mature and responsible behavior, it might just be that the temptations are fewer. Even their characteristic tendency to reminisce (in one family dubbed "reminuisance") is noticeably relieved. Incidentally, churches can be of help in locating suitable foster homes for the aged.

Amazingly, families will forget even the most obvious things about personal contacts when those contacts are fogged with resentments and bickerings. They neglect, for instance, to express approval of things the old folks do and to give encouragement to them as needed. With hired employees they would seldom forget the importance of encouragement — why, then, with Grandpa? Or those issues that loom so large in arguments — what about them? Can they not agree about the children's discipline and its standard so as to avoid tiffs? And is that broken saucer important enough to risk an altercation with a loved one? Emotions play into relationships so intricately that people become unable at times to separate their family's needs from their own angry feelings.

When the pastor is called upon to adjudicate a quarrel in the multi-generation family, he will have to help the family to understand their feelings if reconciliation is to be reached. When our resentments arise, and at times this cannot be helped, it is well to count slowly and review what it is that has really made for anger. Is it some inappropriate act of Grandma's, or is intolerance at the bottom of it all? At times it is necessary to remind the younger people that Grandma has spent a lifetime acquiring the very habits she is exhibiting, and that now she is once again in a period of adjustment. In that adjustment period, doesn't she deserve at least as much understanding as adolescents get in their turbulent adjustment? And Uncle Jake's daily ramblings around town — what's so objectionable about them? When the family stop to think about it, it may be that they fear less his being injured at a street crossing than the inconvenience and care they would have if he should meet with an accident. As a result they continue to frustrate his ambition and independence because they fear that their own comfort may be jeopardized.

Age Should Bring Satisfaction

All the literature on the subject of the aging stresses that older people require meaningful activity if they are to maintain mental health. The classic picture of Whistler's mother sitting serenely with folded hands is charming; but it is also the epitome of boredom. Older people of today are involved in interesting and productive projects. Those who lack the stimulation of outside interests, or who are not well enough to enjoy them, are generally among the unhappy oldsters of the community. The dread of Aunt Catherine in the play *Marty* is expressed well:

"It's gonna happen to you. Mark it well. These terrible years. I'm afraida look inna mirror. I'm afraid I'm gonna see an old lady with white hair, like the old ladies inna park, little bundles inna black shawl, waiting for the coffin. I'm fifty-six years old. What am I to do with myself? I have strength in my hands. I wanna cook. I wanna clean. I wanna make dinner for my children. I wanna be of use to somebody. Am I an old dog to lie in fronta the fire till my eyes close? These are terrible years, Theresa! Terrible years!" (*Television Plays,* by Paddy Chayefsky, p. 156.)

Remunerative work is highest on the list of preferred activities for aged people. If they do not have to retire, or if they can continue in a part-time job for additional income, they feel their age much less. In retirement jobs, some people take on lighter work that resembles the experience they previously had. Thus a real-estate broker may do appraising; a newspaper reporter, free-lance writing; a custodian, small repair jobs. Some, on the other hand, seek new experiences: a college professor accepts a position on the police force as a crossing officer near a grade school and makes friends with hundreds of boys and girls. A maintenance engineer retires to his two-acre lot and raises tulip bulbs to sell. Some list themselves for jury duty, hire out as sitters, or do part-time clerical work. Other quite fortunate individuals have no need for additional income after retirement, but have a yearning to continue to use their talents constructively. Some such people have become dollar-a-year men in welfare, social, or religious organizations. There their penchant for office management, promotion, or finances is appreciated while being utilized to the full.

In many areas there is no end to the amount of voluntary community service one can offer. The American Red Cross solicits the service of women as Gray Ladies. Church, lodge, and civic associations are ever seeking personnel to man numerous committees. Leadership is needed in recreation, crafts, teaching, and in so many different ways that the retired man or woman with a talent can usually find the place to use it.

Educational courses also rank high with our senior citizens as ways of keeping their minds alive. High school, college courses that they never had a chance to take, trade courses, Bible study, and languages attract them in increasing numbers these days. Grandpa Martin was miserable, spending his widowed years in the home of his daughter and making her family almost as unhappy as himself. Then he was approached by an old business associate about learning Spanish in a night school course, and found himself enrolling. He soon discovered he was not too old to learn, nor too old to plan a trip to South America next summer — with a chance to earn part of his expenses by representing an import firm in his home town.

Hobbies can be overrated as therapy in the lives of retired oldsters. A former corporation president does not compensate for his empty days with a butterfly collection. A metropolitan high school principal doesn't find immediate employment in knitting mittens. But hobbies can have amazing therapeutic benefits within limits. In addition, some hobbies can be of financial value. A man who has always played with photography can now earn pocket money by printing films for his friends. A woman whose cakes are the rage of the neighborhood can take orders for her specialties and gain some income from parties and special occasions when her cakes are needed. Hobbies, moreover, have a way of keeping the hands busy when otherwise they might lie motionless in the lap. Hobbies can keep attention occupied when it could be pulled back into grieving for a beloved husband. In the leisure of retirement, it is possible to give more time to interesting hobbies than ever was previously available; and the alert church will open ways for hobbyists to get together.

As a matter of fact, for the type of person who likes people and likes to be with them, the church offers much. Not only in the worship and Bible classes of the church, but also in its more specialized ministry there is increasingly a place for the aged. Groups for our older persons have been organized in many parishes, not to segregate them to be among only those of their own age, but in order to give them opportunity occasionally to be among people of like interests and inclinations. These social groups have played an important part in the well-being of many retired people. The church, moreover, has a need for warm, outgoing persons to make calls on their shut-ins and new people in the community. For this some of our older people are marvelously equipped. In addition, church building committees are at last beginning to take thought of oldsters as they lay plans for stairs, toilet facilities, and doorways, making allowance for aging people's physical problems.

But the church is of vast aid in less material ways. The fellowship of faith undergirds and strengthens its members so that they find more meaning in life, and more purpose. In the historic belief to which the church fellowship attests, we find confidence and hope. For that faith is the epitome of good news; and it emphasizes that we are not alone: underneath are the everlasting arms. In the loneliness and depression so evident among some older people, a living faith will serve as strength. To know the love of God that passes knowledge is to clasp securely one sure anchor when so much else is changing. Nor is this a counsel only for the aged. Both they and their families can place their trust in God in Christ, and find both peace and courage for troublesome days.

Money and the Aged Person

Among the causes of tension in family circles, none is mentioned more often than money. In the case of the older person, the money question is often acute. Invariably his resources are less than what they once were. Savings must be used, and always there is a fear that he may outlive his money and become a pauper. Some have annuity income. Others have pensions from their lifetime work. Most older American citizens now receive Social Security payments; and some are entitled to old-age assistance funds. Yet the Church also needs to review a practice that alienates numerous aged people from services. This is nothing less than that sacrosanct ritual, the offering. If, as in the Society of Friends, funds could be given by subscription, and if the churches were willing to forgo the symbolism involved, more older persons might find their way to common worship.

In an era of slowly increasing enlightenment, employers are less rigid about compulsory retirement at age sixty-five. Many workers are able to continue work, sometimes on a part-time basis, into their senior years. This adds to their mental and financial security so that they exhibit fewer worries and, incidentally, are easier to live with. But the typical case of an older person in the home is that of a person who is no longer gainfully employed. This unemployment may be the very reason for doubling up in the home. Often Grandpa wants to pay his way, but is scarcely able. Many families testify that it is a happier arrangement to allow Grandpa's board and room to be gratis so that he can use his small pension in some way that pleases him — buying something special, or treating them to something they've long wanted and could not afford. He feels more independent this way and the family is not in the position of claiming most of his income for necessities and then doling out special allowances to him for clothing and personal items.

But whatever the plan for finances, it should be settled before Grandpa moves in. These are the decisions best made in a family council, and hammered out through discussion. They can later be modified and improved with mutual experience, but the understandings should be clear beforehand so that there does not arise the complaint, " But no one ever led me to expect this. . . ."

The Need for Privacy

Time-honored tradition in New England provided a special apartment in the family home for the aged members. This was the southwest corner, where the sun is brighter and its rays warmer. Something of that sort needs to be worked out today for those families who have oldsters living with them. Older persons need privacy and a space they can call their own. They need more than a mere bedroom, if that is possible — a sitting room, or perhaps a den or workshop too. They need a place unencumbered by stairs or heights that demand extra energy and make hazards for accidents. The New York State Joint Legislative Committee on Problems of the Aging found that surprisingly little was necessary in special accouterments for older folks' housing. A low bathtub with safety handles, freedom from heights and steps, a comfortable living space, and, for cooking facilities, an electric stove rather than a gas range: these were all that were required for safety and comfort.

Sometimes these facilities are to be found in the home of a son's or daughter's family, and sometimes in other places. Sometimes living space is available in foster homes, financed by the boarders at rates according to their paying ability and supervised by a social work agency. At times the rates are paid by the social agency when neither the elderly person nor his family is able to meet the costs. Institutions for the aged, such as the Church-sponsored homes, have long stood as the traditional solution for the lonely aged. Many of them are located in beautiful surroundings and are supervised carefully for the highest standards. In addition to these are nursing homes for the ill, new units for older people provided in public housing, and the public-sponsored institutions. The great numbers of older persons, however, live alone or with their families.

Living alone can be a depressing routine, going through the daily hours without the companionship of a spouse now gone and missed. There come some days for the idle when it seems not worth-while even to get out of bed! It is then that these persons greatly need the healing benefit of activity, work, and responsibility. When illness comes, the caller from the church is an important tonic. The visiting nurse who comes in, bathes the patient, and does a few services, cheers the apartment. Social agencies also have begun to engage housekeepers who do cooking and house cleaning on occasional visits (sometimes one hour a day, sometimes several days a week).

Often when the first shock of bereavement comes, the family solicitously rush in to say: "Father, you just can't continue to live at this old place any longer. Come in with us and have a family again." Experience demonstrates that it is better to wait longer and get used to the new life before making such decisions. A short delay might prevent an ill-advised move. There is no denying that when the older person moves in with his family, his independence is sacrificed, and he is restricted in ways he had not previously known. Now he can so easily get into the way of teen-agers and their plans, annoy his daughter in her housekeeping, and lose self-assurance in the bargain. Reflect that he is not long on self-assurance at this time anyway because retirement itself, coupled with the death of a lifelong spouse, has been a serious blow to his integrity. Misunderstandings and tensions occur quite naturally in the best of families, and they will come in the three-generation household too. Ironically, sometimes these misunderstandings result from the misapplied kindness of the family. Dr. Walter C. Alvarez says that he has given serious thought to the founding of a Society for the Prevention of Cruelty to Aged Parents by Oversolicitous Children.

When doubling up becomes necessary, it is wise for the family to call a council and talk over the new arrangements so that everyone has a voice in the decision. Does this involve schedules, bathroom arrangements, eating adjustments, changes in furniture, rooms, or routine? Everyone will feel better for knowing the necessary plans. It saves feelings. A three-generation family can be as unified, it is said, as a three-layer cake. But it takes some doing. Dr. George Lawton, an expert in geriatrics, estimates the odds of mutual happiness for an older person among in-laws at one chance in a hundred. To beat those odds requires patience and courtesy.

Perhaps it is best to expect problems, for they will certainly come. An older person uprooted from surroundings, or left with decreasing numbers of friends, might become irritable and ill-adjusted. Being expected to change lifelong patterns to suit a career daughter's apartment, or to compete for attention among young people, is a large order. Not unnaturally, unfavorable reactions set in. The older person desperately needs, as all of us do, a sense of belonging, a feeling of being accepted. But the oldster has much to offer too. He has something to give to family life — a link with the past, stories of the family, a sense of continuity, the stability that grows out of experience, the patience that comes with the years, a philosophy of life.

The family who know what they are doing can work out the living arrangements of an older person happily. It takes intelligence, patience, and something that has historically been known as Christian love.

II. The Handicapped in Families

In an Eastern city several years ago, a father took his young daughter across the fairway of a golf course on their customary morning walk. The child lurched along as always, for she was retarded and unable to walk gracefully. The father remained, as usual, slightly behind her so that he could watch her and help if needed. But today there was one difference. In his hand he carried a small revolver. As the staggering child stepped over the brow of a hill, a shot rang out, and then another.

The bodies of father and daughter were found close together

in death, tragically testifying to the problem of retardation in one family. This man, a church officer, had reached the end of his ability to cope with the problem and had used this way out. The community was shocked. The church was forced into hard thinking: what had it neglected that it might have done to minister to this family?

Today, the problem of mental retardation, of any handicap in fact, is being handled better by an awakening nation. Among those who have helped to bring about this belated change are the clergymen and laymen whose compassion reaches out to the bewildered and the unfortunate. With some three hundred mentally handicapped babies born daily, it is obvious that this condition is far more prevalent than a once-reticent public thought. No less than ten million persons (parents, siblings, and the like) are directly affected by mental retardation, the National Association for Retarded Children estimates.

The alert pastor who finds this project among his parish duties (and no pastor escapes the problem) can help through a series of important steps:

1. He can help parents understand something of the causes of congenital handicaps. There is now an authoritative list of more than seventy diseases or mishaps occurring either before or during birth, or in early childhood, that can produce handicaps. To understand something of these is to be prepared for intelligent counseling.

2. More important, though, he can help them to work through their theological questions, so guilt-laden and vexing. Inevitable as it seems to be, it is completely useless for the parent to bemoan his fate and ask, "What did I ever do to deserve this?" To presume that the handicap of a child must be the punishment of a parent's own sin presents a gross caricature of God. When this same false notion was broached about the blind man, according to John, ch. 9, Jesus clarified the issue. Someone had asked, "Master, who did sin, this man, or his parents, that he was born blind?" Jesus answered, "Neither hath this man sinned, nor his parents: but that the works of God should be made manifest in him." Then Jesus healed him. Once again the need of man had

become the opportunity for God's grace.

Great danger lies in self-blame or in seeking scapegoats. A mother may probe into her background, regretting that she took this medicine or consulted that doctor. A father may blame himself for some past error, or perhaps even for marrying at all. The upshot of such self-torture too often is that parents fall to squabbling between themselves and then take it out on the child, unwittingly punishing him for their own insecurities and guilt. Unexplained though these misfortunes often are, they can occur in any family. Perhaps four fine healthy children are born into a home, and then an idiot. The difficulty may be traced to a hormone deficiency, to German measles in a mother-to-be, or to scores of other causes, perhaps only to mystery. What is important is not to fix blame, but to take steps to help the child and the family.

3. The pastor can help parents to understand their own feelings. A deaf or lame child has fears; for every affliction has its terrors. If, at times, the youngster becomes frustrated and tearful, it should cause no surprise. If then the parents at times are impatient or irritable, it is natural. If the minister acknowledges that a feeling of resentment in such a case is normal and understandable, it goes a long way toward helping parents to bear their burden.

4. But the clergyman need not stop there. In his pastoral care he can help families to work through their feelings about a handicapped member. They can be led not only to accept the undeniable facts as facts but also *to accept him as a person*. The pastor's assistance in thinking through decisions about institutional or home care may be needed in many a long, soul-searching conversation. His pastoral calling upon the family may be urgently needed to maintain morale. His interpretation of handicaps to the congregation can help an entire church to understand a vicious problem.

5. If in addition he teams up with physicians and psychiatrists to help families, more progress can be made. Further, he can accomplish much if in prayer he remembers these families among his intercessions and lays their need upon the goodness of God.

6. In church organization work, still other contributions can be made. The compassionate church will establish special church school classes for these exceptional children, teaching them simply and patiently. Such congregations have inaugurated play schools, parents' groups for those who share this problem, day care nurseries, and social groups for retarded teen-agers. Efforts have been made (and found successful) to nurture whole churches in sympathetic regard toward the handicapped — integrating retarded people into the life of the church wherever possible, building or remodeling facilities with the limitations of the handicapped as a consideration, and raising a corps of leaders to teach and help handicapped individuals. When church people begin to accept the handicapped, the morale of the families of the handicapped is also lifted. As their understanding and acceptance grows, families see new possibilities for their handicapped children. One such father, cheerful and aware, regarded his son's limited vocational prospects, and concluded, "But the world needs good shoeshine men too, Pastor."

Perhaps the summary word to this subject can best be spoken by Roman Catholic Archbishop Cushing, who at the dedication of St. Coletta's Chapel in Jefferson, Wisconsin, said that we are also among those who ask: "'Master, how shall we explain all this? Whose sin was it? The children's? Their parents'? Ours?' and He tells us: They are neither punishments nor pointless. The point is that God has a work to do through exceptional children — exceedingly important work, exceptionally important. It is fair to say that the best index to the civilization of a community is what is done for exceptional children, for they are usually least in so many ways: least in years, least in endowments, least in privileges; least in all the things that people covet for their children. For as much as ye have done it to the least of these, ye have done it unto me."

III. Pastoral Care of Childless Couples

The classic plight of Sarah, of Rachel, and of Hannah in Old Testament literature is also known to thousands of women today.

Inability to conceive a child is to them a heavy sorrow, for their entire psychophysical structure is geared by creation to child-bearing. When this proves impossible, a burden of grief, or guilt, or bitterness can result. It may not be any consolation at all in such marriages to quote Karl Barth's theological point that for them *the* child has already been born. What they ardently want is a baby of their own.

Not infrequently such couples come to their pastors to seek some guidance in their problem; and he should know something of the nature of infertility and the grounds for hope now avail-able in medical science. Other things being equal, data show that the earlier the physician gets to work on a case of sterility, the better the chance for its correction. When a husband and wife have attempted for more than a year to conceive a child and still remain unsuccessful, they ought to seek medical help. The correction may be simple and swift, or it may take a long time, but early therapy is essential. The husband is first examined to ascertain whether there are too few spermatozoa in his semen. His general health, as well as his history of disease (mumps and venereal infection have often caused sterility in the male), is carefully checked. If he is found to be capable of fatherhood, attention next turns to the more difficult and involved examina-tion of the wife. In the wife's examination, the physician seeks to learn whether her pelvic organs are normal, and whether there is any malformation of the ovaries. Sometimes a tubal ligation is effective in clearing up the difficulty. Sometimes hormone treat-ment will overcome " cervical hostility " to sperm.

In other cases, counseling is found to be therapeutic because psychogenic factors play an influential though elusive part in the process. Morris Fishbein's *Children for the Childless* notes that the very act of seeking medical advice at a sterility clinic often leads to conception before treatment has been begun. " It is pre-sumed that the very fact that the couple have made up their minds to do something about their problem somehow promotes fertility " (p. 66). The pastor who is acquainted with the nature of infertility and its accompanying problems will want to keep informed about medical resources and clinics in his community, social work agencies and adoption possibilities, and the pros and cons of artificial insemination. When he has read widely and thought deeply, he will still be confronted with the mystery of why more than ten per cent of our population remains infertile. And in his ministry to families he will occasionally have to assist them in making an adjustment to a situation of childlessness. Some of them will not even be able to adopt children because of the great demand for babies; and the pastor will have a task in reconciliation and counseling to perform. For such work he will need to be a man of deep faith and fervent prayer.

How the Pastor Aids in Adoption

In former days, pastors acted as adoption agents, mercifully placing unsanctioned babies with parishioners for rearing. This service, though kind, was performed without meticulous regard for the fitness of the adopting parents, or any scientific concern to locate the most suitable parents for a given child. In such cases too, the advisable legal arrangements were apt to slip by without attention for years.

Now, however, the pastor's role is quite different, and a good thing that is. Clergymen do little child placement, but they assist expert social caseworkers who supervise the adoption of more than 75,000 babies annually. For these 75,000 babies, however, there are at least one million applicants, according to statistics of the Child Welfare League of America. Most of these babies have been born to unwed mothers, who in 1954 were delivered of an estimated 142,000 illegitimate children in the U.S.A. (figures from the U.S. Senate Subcommittee on Juvenile Delinquency). Other factors, however, also lead to placement of children for adoption: death of one or both parents, divorce or separation, chronic illness, or occasionally a prison sentence.

The pastor can be of service at several points in aiding parishioners to find a child. He can first counsel with them about making this important decision, supporting and encouraging their application where he thinks it wise. He can refer them to a reputable and authoritative agency and steer them clear of black-market operations when they apply for a child. He can recommend the applying parents, and serve as a reference on their behalf.

Secondly, he can help them in the long, trying months and years while they wait to secure a child. Placement of adoptable children is an intricate operation, protected in nearly every state by a careful system of regulatory safeguards. These laws will sometimes appear to the would-be parents as frustrating and delaying. But they have been devised for the protection of the child, and indirectly of the adopting parents themselves. Again and again these facts must be interpreted to the couple who wish to adopt, for it can at times seem to them that red tape has been tied up only to annoy them. The agency entrusted with this important function is first of all concerned with the welfare of the child and only secondarily with the hopes of the couple — a fact that they will come to appreciate more fully after the adoption has been completed.

Reputable agencies do a tremendous job of bringing together a child and parents who are suited to each other. They may be local welfare agencies, licensed by the state, or one of the special private groups such as Welcome House at Doylestown, Pennsylvania, where children of Amerasian background are sheltered. In either case, they carefully take down detailed information about the hopeful couple in an application process; they interview the couple not just once but many times over a period of months, and they interview also their references, neighbors, associates, and friends. When they come to interview the pastor, they may be seeking as much to see what kind of home his is as to learn what he thinks about the couple. The reason for this is that they can tell indirectly some things about the couple by seeing the kind of family life their references have.

The process of interviewing, checking references, and studying the children to be adopted is a long waiting period. It seems interminable to those who wait, and often stretches into two years or more. But finding suitable homes for the children that are available calls for meticulous, detailed work. The agencies check health, intelligence, personality traits, and other pertinent factors before coming to a decision. Seldom is it feasible to assign the first baby that becomes available. It may be, for instance, that that child has an intelligence quotient too limited to expect him ever to be college material; and it might be unwise therefore to place him in a home with college-educated parents who expect that their intellectual standards are to be the norm for their children.

The pastor will one day hear that the agency has called to ask the applicants to come to visit the child. He will have been kept in a foster home for some time previous and brought to the agency to be seen by the applicants. Their reactions now are the key to decision. Will they accept this child whom the agency recommends for them? In most cases they do and the pastor can rejoice with them. The social worker relates essential facts about the child's background and endowment. (Adopting parents should keep this information to themselves; it is not for family and friends.) In case of infant adoption, the social worker often holds back one piece of information, shielding the identification of the blood parents. This secrecy holds also for the adopting parents in most cases in order to prevent them ever from being confronted by the blood mother in some heartbreaking moment of remorse. Later if the grown child may wish to search out his real parents, he should not be restrained or ridiculed in it. Certainly the adoptive parents need not feel offended if this very natural desire is manifested. Rather, they would be wise to permit him to go back to the agency and make inquiry. The agency personnel know from frequent experience how to handle this visit without disclosing too much, and afterward everyone concerned will feel better about the situation.

Pastoral care extends through the period that precedes adoption also to the post-adoption years. From the very beginning the pastor may be called upon at a number of points. The pastor can help interpret to the parents what is involved in adopton procedures. For this purpose, he will find useful *How to Adopt a Child,* by Ernest and Frances Cady. A brief ten-cent pamphlet from the Children's Bureau entitled *When You Adopt a Child* (Children's Bureau Folder 13–1947 from the Government Printing Office, Washington 25, D.C.) uses simple, reassuring words to inform a couple of the realities of adopting a baby: " His coming to your home will mean one of the biggest changes your life ever had. That you want to cuddle him is fine. But never forget that that little blue or pink bundle you hold is a human being. . . . It's a *mighty* serious business. It needs a lot of thinking through. And it has its pitfalls, its hazards, its risks: not only for you but for the baby or child you will be taking into your home."

Frequently the wondering couple will ask themselves and their pastor whether they could possibly love someone else's child as if he were their own. The reply is straightforward and assuring: this same question is asked by most applicants, and universal experience is that they do love their adopted child with the same depth and ardor of any human parent. This reply, of course, must satisfy emotionally as much as intellectually, if it is to convince; and sometimes it is believable only when it has been experienced.

When adoption papers have been completed, usually about six months after the child has moved into the home, the " trial period " has passed and the court (or agency) is satisfied that the arrangement is good. The parents' lawyer will arrange with the court to complete the papers (certainly not outside the state of their residence lest they become involved in legal problems they would rather avoid). The pastor is advised to become familiar with his local laws and agency practices because they differ among the states. To gain such information he can visit a social caseworker of the community and learn the facts he needs, as well as locate a useful ally for future contacts about social problems; for the social worker is an exceedingly valuable colleague to any minister in his parish work. These social workers and their agencies carry through with adoptive parents at every step of the process.

When the adoption is accomplished, the pastor's work is not finished. He will be needed again. To aid the new parents in making the child at home in a loving, accepting relationship is all-important; and this element of Christian parent education cannot be neglected. The parent-child problems from here on are not different from those of any other family, with two notable exceptions: (1) The necessity of telling the child quite early in his life about his adoption. This can be done gradually, easily, and matter-of-factly, and must be performed by the adoptive parents themselves lest he learn the facts from someone else and be hurt through the experience. (A useful tool for this purpose is the two-volume set *The Adopted Family,* by Florence Rondell and Ruth Michaels. This charming story can be read aloud to the child so that he will understand. (2) The other exception involves the emotional control of the adopting parents. They must be helped to see that they should never mention the matter of adoption in time of anger or pique lest the child feel unwanted. He may feel rejected and may fear that he would be returned to some unknown place that is not home. Such a misfortune would be regretted by all parties concerned for years to come, and ought never to occur.

But suppose the wistful couple in the church are not selected by the agency to receive a baby. What then? They may be deemed too old for the agency policy. Usually it is worked out that an adopting couple have growing children approximately at the age they would have had children of their own growing up. This prevents the awkward situation that can obtain when a seventy-year-old father has a fifteen-year-old boy, and is too far from him both in understanding and energy to enjoy him. Unlike German adoption laws that require the adoptive father to be fifty, or Swiss law' that makes the minimum age for adoptive parents forty, American standards match young children with young parents. This appears wise from what we have learned about parents and children growing together.

The couple deemed too old to adopt an infant can nonetheless be encouraged to look into adopting an older child of six, nine, or eleven. Junior-age children are frequently passed by in demand for little babies. Yet school-age children may be more easily found than small babies. New legislation enacted in 1953 by Congress authorized 4,500 nonquota visas for children of other lands to be adopted by American parents (Public Laws 162 and 203). From these contacts also come growing children available for adoption, but it must be added that administration of the law has been confusing, and some Americans have abused the plan shamelessly, accepting foreign children only to ship them back again by plane when they did not suit them.

There may be other reasons than age that makes the agency find the applicants unacceptable. It may be that they feel guilty or deprived because of infertility and seek a child for their ego needs. Or they may seek a baby to save a slipping marriage — a plan that is never wise. Some women may seek a child as a new antidote to neurotic illness, or to avoid normal birth because of their fears about labor. Such reasons are suspect; and the minister who senses that such bases underlie adoption ambitions need not be dismayed when an agency rejects their application.

Foster homes are urgently needed for many children who are not available for adoption. Often these are the children of widows who temporarily cannot keep them, or of parents who are ill, separated, or declared by a court incompetent to retain them. The Church can perform a noteworthy service to the community in finding foster parents to house such children for temporary care. Often this involves a nominal stipend from county welfare funds that eases the financial burden. Whether the foster family require an allowance or not, they are ofttimes the means of keeping a worthy child from delinquency, and providing him even temporarily with wholesome home life.

In his ministry to church families, the pastor will carry a continuing concern that childless couples are not cruelly hurt by the jests or thoughtless remarks of other church members. If in his own attitude toward them, and in his preaching and educational work he is compassionate and understanding, church members will begin to fall into the same pattern of compassionate regard. However, the greatest opportunity he has to enlarge a congregation's empathy for the childless is in the way that he assists in adoption proceedings. This truly is a pastoral ministry to church families.

The Question of Artificial Insemination

So far, artificial insemination has proved too controversial a subject for most Church bodies. The National Council of

Churches attempted a statement several years ago, but were unable to reach any consensus among the many Protestant opinions there represented. The Church of England appointed a scholarly commission to study the question, but to their thorough report is appended a minority opinion by the Dean of St. Paul's Cathedral taking issue with most of the conclusions. Even the Church of Rome seems unsettled by the question; their *Medico-Moral Problems,* Part II (edited by Gerald Kelly, S.J.) contains a number of italicized paragraphs in later editions that cite the pope's corrections, now making earlier statements in this series "historically interesting but not solidly probable."

Artificial insemination of humans is not new. Earliest case histories point to a successful attempt about 175 years ago in London; but this system has been known in animal husbandry for centuries. However, in this scientific era when the practice is no longer so novel, and its effects far more profound, it has come in for additional attention in magazine articles, social casework, medical practice, and theological disputations.

The theory is rather simple. When a fertile wife is unable to conceive, she can be assisted by a gynecologist, who places semen directly in the cervix. During her ovulation period, several such treatments are given and in a very high percentage of cases (estimated at 97 per cent) conception takes place. When the semen is that of the husband, collected for this purpose and introduced into the vaginal canal by artificial means because some physical condition of his prevents as effective an introduction in intercourse, there are few objections except from the Roman Catholics, who associate this with the sin of onanism. However, when the semen is collected from a donor who is not the husband, a host of ethical questions present themselves and clamor for attention.

Those who favor artificial insemination by an anonymous donor point out arguments in its favor: (1) In cases where the husband is infertile, this situation at least makes an experience of maternity possible for his wife, and half of the baby's genes come from the family — something not true of adoption; (2) the operation is carried out in complete secrecy so that the donor's name is never known to the parents, nor theirs to him, thus preventing any unusual emotional attachments or resentments among the principals involved; and even the obstetrician who later cares for the mother and the child's delivery has no knowledge of the infant's origin; (3) it is estimated that in the U.S.A. one in eight couples is infertile, and artificial insemination by means of a donor presents the couple with a possibility of parenthood; (4) it is possible to mix the semen of the husband with that of the donor before the insemination takes place, thereby opening the possibility that it was the husband after all who is the father; (5) an estimated 50,000 births have already taken place by this means (and this very probably is an exceedingly low estimate), so the practice is already widely accepted and in general use; (6) some women have an indescribably strong desire not just to adopt a child but to bear a child of their own, and this method opens up that possibility.

Legislation has begun to cover the legal problems involved. Bills that would declare the artificially inseminated life as legitimate have been introduced into the legislatures of Wisconsin, New York, Minnesota, and Virginia. The New York City Department of Health has established a code of careful regulations for physicians in artificial insemination work. Yet the courts are still uncertain about the legal status of such children. Laws concerning legitimacy and bastardy were drawn up before the practice of artificial insemination became common; and they fail to cover this exigency. As a result, a judge in Chicago declared a child illegitimate and the mother an adulteress in one divorce case, and a judge in New York delivered an opposite opinion in a similar case before him. English law has been even more conservative in declaring *all* such children as illegitimate, thereby prevented from receiving any inheritance from the family line.

It is not the legal considerations so much as the ethical and theological that interest the pastor. When a couple in his church seek his counsel on this question, what is he to say? Fraught with uncertainty as the question now is, there are still some principles that to me seem determinative.

1. Artificial insemination by means of a donor is technically

adultery, no matter how we look at it. To declare that it is not because the personal element is missing, and because no carnal pleasure is involved misses the point. Insisting that only those experiences are sinful that are enjoyable is the kind of sophistry occasionally found in a perversion of Calvinism.

2. So far, most of the arguments in behalf of artificial insemination are based upon the cases where a woman is capable of producing children, but her husband is not. Suppose that the next step were to consider the converse condition, where a husband is fertile and his wife is not. Would we then expect to support a new system whereby he would make his spermatozoa available for artificial insemination into some fecund woman's uterus and then have that infant brought into his home for rearing? Here the situation becomes more complicated; the questions are even tougher as they touch on security feelings, jealousy, and marital relationships.

3. Is there not something specious in the tacit assumption that child-bearing makes for a bond in marriage but that infertility cannot? Every pastor is acquainted with childless couples who have borne their yearning as a shared burden, and have found that in the process they grew closer together.

4. Indeed, those who are concerned about marital health in our time will want to think carefully about the long-run effects on marriage as an institution if artificial insemination by anonymous donors becomes common. There is an impersonal factor here which can be destructive — " She's my child, but not yours! " has been angrily alleged in divorce suits. The opportunity for subsequent conflict between husband and wife, or even the stepfather and child, cannot be ruled out.

5. At the time of their marriage, each couple promised to forsake all others as long as they both should live. Yet for them later to agree that a third party, not known to them, shall be the seed for their children is bringing another into the relationship in a dramatic and not easily justifiable way. In this act their one-flesh union is violated; and that effect upon Christian marriage needs painstaking examination.

6. Apart from these considerations there is the question of the

donor himself. It has been averred that he is hypothetically capable of fathering thousands of children by means of his semen, frozen in semen banks and divided into portions for numerous inseminations. What this possibility does to the man himself in encouraging pride or a Mr. Adam complex is difficult to conjecture. That it presents at least the theoretical possibility of half-siblings later marrying each other is undeniably possible. Moreover, there is the chilling realization that such power in the hands of a eugenically minded dictator, such as Adolf Hitler was, could have international implications and make for a race of hybrid people in some "brave new world." As a matter of actual fact, in 1945 the House Military Affairs Committee received the proposal that test-tube babies be produced to guard the atom-bomb secrets of America, and that the parents be chosen by eugenicists to populate the strategic laboratories of the nation so as to have the best brains in the world to control future atomic power! (*Artificial Human Insemination,* London, S.P.C.K., 1948, p. 33.)

7. Unmarried women who have as strong a desire to bear babies as their wedded sisters can present a convincing case for their own insemination by donors also. A League of Bachelor Mothers already exists in England, and has publicly issued a statement attesting to their right to have such children without marriage. In a day when the family is already threatened by a spate of hostile attacks, this one has sobering ramifications indeed.

The issue is far from settled. It can be predicted that the case for artificial insemination by donation from professional donors will grow in popularity as the scientific techniques improve. Already, frozen semen has been flown long distances by air to impregnate women in distant countries. Semen banks, patterned after our blood banks, have been proposed for tomorrow's needs. The Margaret Sanger Research Bureau has been at work on new possibilities in artificial human insemination. Some medical men now specialize in this one field. A recent motion picture, *Fruit Without Love,* was produced in Germany dealing with the theme. In one Gallup poll, 24 per cent of the men, 31 per cent of the women, approved of test-tube babies. Joseph Fletcher in his

Morals and Medicine approves not only of the plan, but also of telling the child of his origin, just as in cases of adoption. The whole question cries for urgent study by Church groups so that pastors and Christian couples can be guided through this maze with more certainty.

In all this attention, too little is said about the alternatives to artificial, donated insemination. The suggestion that each person receive a premarital fertility examination is taken seriously by too few couples. It would open the way to earlier therapy for sterility, and might be the means of correcting many a condition of infertility that now persists too long. Adoption also is far more satisfactory for families than proponents for artificial insemination seem willing to admit. Even care of foster children offers many satisfactions to families, and it does not compromise the marriage bond by an artificial situation that threatens the essential character and purpose of the home.

8

THE PASTOR
AS A FAMILY MAN

If a man does not know how to manage
his own household, how can he care
for God's church? — Paul, in his First Letter to Timothy
(ch. 3:5).

Protestant philosophy, sound and proven, has decreed that to be
an effective pastor the minister ought also to be a disciplined individual who has come to terms with life's most intimate relationship — the family. The minister who has made a mature
adjustment in marriage (" the husband of one wife "), as well as
in fatherhood (who does not " provoke his children to wrath "),
will be the more adequate in his pastoral work. For years the
manse has been a school for Christian living, rearing tomorrow's
clergymen and future clergymen's wives. Many a minister has
seen his family life to be what Martin Luther called it, *larva Dei,*
(a mask of God) through which God's grace and goodness are
revealed. Where that family life has been genuine and loving
and considerate, where a Christian spirit permeates through the
family, theirs becomes a home that blesses all who enter it. It
would be deceitful, however, to infer that because the clergyman
in his professional life is an interpreter of the Christian faith, it
follows easily that his home life will be felicitous and secure. It
may happen indeed that professional life is at odds with his family life and makes that relationship harder.

The pastor is a man set apart; and his uniqueness affects his
family relationships. He is the man to whom people apologize
when they inadvertently drop a cuss word. In correspondence
he is addressed formally as "Reverend Sir." He holds down a

job that, like no other on earth, demands the whole man. However, when he is at home he is not the clergyman, but a person. Although there are occasions when he must minister to the people of his own home, here his role is different. He learns the truth of Anatole France's word that it is difficult to be a saint in the midst of one's family. He has children whose opinions conflict with his own about their dates, friends, and activities. He feels the pain of family mutiny on those occasions when they rebel against demands of attendance at and participation in institutional religion. He knows the effect of fatigue upon family relationships. Yet if he fails here in his own home, it may well be that no amount of vocational success will ever make up for it.

George Hedley, in *The Minister Behind the Scenes* (p. 143), quotes a letter written by a mother to her son at college, in which she offered her reasons why he should consider the ministry as his life's work: "The work is easy, the social status good, and you don't really have to believe in God." A quite different view is that of the idolizing parishioner who with starry eyes sees the clergyman as a kind of demigod, very nearly to be worshiped by an adoring congregation. Both views are equally ridiculous; and no one knows it as well as the parson's family. Whatever may be the misunderstanding of society about him as a whole, at home the pastor is known for the man he is. No professional pose can last long in the manse; it will soon have to be dropped somewhere in the give-and-take of family relations. If he devotes all his time and his energy to making a success of his profession, life in the manse must suffer. He may, by reason of industrious work and long hours, become known for his prowess as a minister of distinction; but it is possible for him to gain a church and to lose a home.

Astonishingly, though, some pastors lack sufficient understanding of family life either to enjoy it themselves or to help parishioners with theirs. Sometimes they have been so busy in work for the Kingdom and so aloof from family living that they show far less comprehension of family dynamics than do the laity. In spite of this, denominational boards and agencies habitually address family education materials to the pastor for automatic transmission to his congregation. In certain few cases this is as logical as engaging a pacifist to teach combat tactics to Marine recruits. Paul's words can be addressed to these parsons who live outside their homes: "If a man does not know how to manage his own household, how can he care for God's church?" The fitness of a pastor to assume the cure of souls is roughly proportionate to his quality as a husband and father. Wayne E. Oates in his book *The Christian Pastor* (p. 51) puts the problem in proper frame: "Real question may be raised as to the sincerity of a . . . [minister] who uses his Christian calling as an excuse to neglect the basic physical and emotional needs of his children. If a man neglects his own children's need for affectionate tenderness, spiritual instruction, and economic security, he will have no basis for a genuinely pastoral care of the flock of God." The damning accusation of one daughter of the manse is perhaps too typical: "Dad is so busy going places and giving speeches on family life that we never see him around the house."

Pressures on the Manse

As any pastor knows, his family is beset by most of the problems that attack any other family in modern civilization, but by several more in addition. They are not immune to the usual tensions of financial pressures, personal failure, and contention; but they have others peculiar to the profession. In some communities clergymen's families still live in a goldfish bowl. Lessened though this trial now is, the community's surveillance of the manse and their expectations of perfection in the clergyman's family can become a nearly unbearable burden. The heavy obligation of social, administrative, and ministerial functions has made tense abodes of some manses, while the imposition of church life on the home of the pastor has sometimes threatened the peaceful quality of family living that had been there.

The testimony of one college girl, in *Parent and Child*, by James H. S. Bossard, tells why she has long since made up her mind that *she* would never marry a minister. The manse that was her home was a veritable public house. Parishioners walked in without knocking, drove by unexpectedly to show the house to their friends, abruptly came to borrow anything they desired or required. Still and all, she had to admit that there were advantages in her home too: the inspiring presence of outstanding guests, the unusual prestige accorded her family, the cultural and educational contacts they enjoyed. Vaguely she realized that manse life, for all its pressures and inconveniences, develops a remarkable depth of family devotion and loyalty. But the fact remains that many clergy families never know what it is to have a quiet telephone, to ease community pressure off their children, to enjoy a life without the kinds of demands and impositions that create new problems and require constant adjustments. No pastors' homes are immune to the internal tensions that feed upon the anxieties and worries of parsons who are too concerned about how their households appear to the parishioners. Manse families know all too well the devilish goadings C. S. Lewis describes in *The Screwtape Letters:* " mutual annoyance, daily pinpricks " (p. 21).

The pastor rarely spends as much time with his family as he ought, and in later years he may rue the fact that he felt professional duty required so much sacrifice of family relationships. His sense of values needs constant, prayerful review lest he subjugate family welfare to administrivia under the mistaken assumption that these comprise the entire Kingdom of God. If his family suffers from his neglect, it may well be because he has abdicated his rightful place as paterfamilias. As Wesner Fallaw suggests in *Toward Spiritual Security* (pp. 184-185): " An able counselor of long experience has said that he spends a major part of his time with young people whose fathers are professional men. Teachers, professors, parsons, physicians, psychiatrists, social workers, and more — many of whom know the theory of proper child nurture — not infrequently fail as parents. People sometimes point to them not so much in ridicule as by way of discounting their fancy educational and psychological theories. But it is not their theories and knowledge about child care and family relations that are incorrect; what is wrong is that professional men too seldom get around to investing enough time with their families so as to make sound knowledge function."

Congregations will understand, and families will appreciate, a night reserved each week for dates with wife and children. A family night at home for Father and everyone, occasional special trips and treats for pastor and each member of the family, time taken for serious talks: these pay off handsomely. Much of the tension felt by clergymen's families could be relieved by the simple expedient of spending more time together. The busy pastor who is Forging Ahead and Accomplishing Things has to find time somewhere; and he learns early a practical and unfortunate lesson, that the easiest place to steal it is from his family. A pastor in a Chicago church was surprised one Sunday to find a pew card checked at the space that indicated: "Desire pastor to call at my home." It was signed by his own wife. He called all right, and mended his phrenetic ways. Another hard-working pastor spent so much time calling upon prospects for church membership that his family threatened to quit the church membership so that he would also call on them.

While automation clears the way for more and more hours of leisure for the machine worker, it does nothing for the leisure of the clergyman. No machine is yet on the drawing boards that will visit the sick, counsel the disturbed, or administer a church program. In fact, unless he watches carefully, the greater leisure occasioned by automation may cause him a heavier schedule of work. Unless he plans his time so that the family gets something near to normal home life, his greatest pastoral counseling problem may turn up on his own doorstep. The serious pursuits for which our profession is caricatured (Thomas Kelly in *A Testament of Devotion* used to call these "perpetually passing out cold cups of water") can hardly be justified as a good enough reason for neglecting those in our own homes for whose care we are also responsible to God.

However, there is another word to be written about this time problem. The family of a clergyman must understand that his ordination vows demand much of him, and that there do come periods when he is completely occupied away from home, fulfilling his holy vocation. If he gets this point across, the family will resent less his absences and be able also to call him to task more readily when they find him just busy. This allows them to share in his labors, knowing that although he cannot and often will not explain his involvements that he is still fulfilling the ministry to which he is called. It may be that he can never give as much time to his home as can the shift worker; but he does give them something that other families may never know as well — an insight into the glorious and tragic aspects of everyday life, and a vision of the grace that sustains us all.

Many a clergyman needs simply to learn to play with his family; but he also knows that not every type of recreation is good. Mistakenly we sometimes spend large sums on luxurious rest only so that we may later work more strenuously. Sometimes (and pastors excel in this) we maintain with pride that we have no leisure — and any observer might well note that then we also have precious little family life. Unconscious of the drives that impel us, we frequently choose our recreation according to inbred prejudices. The middle-class Protestant family is so conditioned by the Puritan ethic that it may never be wholly comfortable about play for its own sake. We are still capable of viewing children's play as time ill spent unless it be preparation for later life. An entire industry, manufacturing "educational toys," thrives upon this idea. Or we may guiltily consider adult recreation as something for which we must apologize. It is not altogether true, as Sunday supplements often allege, that what families need is to spend more time together. That kind of familiarity has bred contempt as often as it has fostered solidarity. Family recreation, as any tired father will know, can militate against an individual's recreation and/or rest. The enthusiastic plans of recreationists for folk dancing, hiking, or play-reading can at times be menacing to the family's welfare.

We then retreat to the passive kinds of play; and our spectatoritis form of recreation becomes an expression of a yearning for something more exciting than the obligations of our daily life. Vicariously we thrill to the hazards of space travel as we watch a science-fiction film, or shout our throats hoarse while some young man breaks through right tackle for a thirty-yard run. Down deep in our being, each of us wants to spend his life on something bigger than himself. We must confront situations that challenge us in order to feel life is worth-while. Here precisely is where Christianity makes its contribution to our family living, with its historic insistence that God has made us for himself and that our hearts are restless till they find rest in him. The Church is peculiarly fitted to divide the word " recreation " into its component parts, placing emphasis upon the prefix " re." Our families will find with us their re-creation when together we devote ourselves to significant fellowship. No hectic schedule of parish work should be permitted to crowd out of manse life those experiences which help us to build the kind of home life that God meant for us, that even provides an example of happy fellowship to others.

The Pastor as a Father

No father, not even the pastor, can safely abdicate his place in the family for reasons of his profession without suffering for it. His children, who greatly need the guidance of a father, will also suffer. That both a father and a mother are essential to the well-being of a child is a truth that has always been known; but only in recent years have we understood the reasonable psychological basis for this fact. Children need all the guidance that both of their parents can give them. Girls look to their fathers for an example of masculinity, to their mothers for femininity. Boys look to their mothers for an understanding of the feminine role, but to their fathers for an example of manhood. And this process will someday affect their own marriage patterns. Children grow by identifying themselves with their parents. Just as youngsters look to fathers for a pattern of maturity, they observe his values, attitudes, outlook, and faith. They are working out their own philosophy of life, and they learn to live with others by observing how Father and Mother get along together. To give our children enough protection, but not so much that it smothers their development, to communicate to them certainty in this uncertain world, to allow them to gain independence without neglect, calls for a degree of wisdom that not even ministers possess.

It is good that we can look for help to the Father for whom every family in heaven and on earth is named.

Our children need and respect limits to their behavior. They feel more secure when they know how far they may go. And they are most appreciative of discipline when it is administered as a teaching device by parents who themselves are self-disciplined. The father who is essentially a disciplined person finds his children less resentful of his disciplinary procedure than he would if he exhibited no respect for limitations himself. We have come to realize that most childish naughtiness is not a plan to defeat affection on the part of parents, but is exactly the opposite, a fumbling attempt to gain the attention that proves someone cares enough to draw the line. Modern parents provide opportunities for the animal spirits of their bairns to be expressed in something less destructive than ripping up books in the study or crayoning on the walls of the manse. And when the cantankerousness of the child cannot be described as anything other than an attempt to avenge himself against a parent, they seek to learn what it is that has prompted such revenge.

Child-training is not a science, and cannot follow rigid rules. Family relationships must be worked out according to family patterns and the needs of the child. True discipline is a learning experience that need not necessitate pain if it is the preventive type which does its teaching prior to the expected problem. Such a theory takes into account the personality of the child and his own faults, forgiving him when he has failed, helping him to solve problems.

Most of our discipline misunderstandings with children come out of that old bugaboo, projection, and it can reach unusually severe extremes in a pastor. The minister who cannot accept his own child's weaknesses because they seem to reflect painfully upon himself tends to have the greatest trouble. It is when discipline is emphasized as child management, i.e., for the glory or the comfort of the parents, that unchristian and unrealistic factors are brought into play.

In many a manse where there is dissension and trouble, nothing is of greater need than a father who assumes his rightful role as father. Old-fashioned though the concept is, the home of today needs the security that comes from wise authority and well-founded firmness. This does not mean the kind of autocratic authority to which the nineteenth century was accustomed. A book written by Rev. J. N. Danforth in 1844 could describe the home as a palace in which the father is " monarch of that little empire, wearing a crown that is the gift of heaven, swaying a scepter put into his hands by the Father of all, acknowledging no superior, fearing no rival, and dreading no usurper " (*The Token of Friendship, or Home, the Center of Affections*). Today our children would soon set us straight if we tried to pull off a pose as ludicrous as that. Ours is a far more permissive age, in which the family is less an institution than it is a companionship. Yet modern men, and clergymen among them, have abdicated rather more of their masculine authority than is good for them or for their families. Sam Levenson, the television comedian, tells in six simple words why none of the children in his slum-reared family ever became delinquents: "Papa wouldn't have stood for it." It is passing strange that a valiant leader in ecclesiastical affairs, who speaks forth courageously and launches out boldly, often steps down when he is at home and allows the manse to become a matriarchy.

As long as our manse children are confused about the origin of discipline (is it parental convenience, or is it because Father too is under a higher authority?), there remains for them the untenable ethic that "wrong" is something that displeases Father, and that "right" is what they have been admonished to do. They need authority all right, but the authority of Christian love. A mere piety without reference to love simply obligates the children to obey so as to avoid reprisals, but they will not be impressed with the justice of this piety nor be trained well for their own maturity.

It is of no avail to speak of Christian conditioning in home life, or to suggest the "Church in the house" pattern, if the parent lacks authority to exercise discipline of self or progeny. Whatever were the drawbacks of that older Victorian pattern of paternal authoritarianism, it was based upon a sound philosophy. As

Charles Clayton Morrison has noted, it was clumsy and it was harsh, "but with all its faults of method it had the right idea. The idea was to equip the growing child with the language of religion, to impregnate his mind with the lore of the Christian cultus, to put him in possession of his rich heritage as a member of the continuing community of those who serve and worship God." (*The Social Gospel and the Christian Cultus*, p. 77.)

The anxieties that modern parents suffer about child-training are so widespread that they have given rise to a host of literature and educational programs. But such anxiety can be multiplied out of all proportion in the home of a pastor who strives for family perfection in order to gain community approval. Together with many other parents, the pastor may subscribe to the popular myth that unless a child is properly conditioned in the early years of life, he will never be well adjusted at all. It is true that a child's early years find him malleable; and this is a fruitful time for training. But this claim is quite different from saying that if our chances are missed at this time, they can never be recouped.

An extreme group of psychoanalysts have popularized this heresy of determinism until it is widely accepted and frequently repeated by persons whose very own experience belies the theory. Books and articles repeat the canard until it is an accepted folk truth of our culture. True, conditioning *is* powerful, as we have indicated. Yet the whole idea behind education is the expectation that people can be changed. The underlying foundation of all counseling is that conditions and attitudes can be improved from an unpromising start. Our understanding of developmental tasks is that we are capable of considerable alteration in personality and behavior during certain stages of life: marriage, parenthood, climacteric, et cetera. Dr. Milton Senn's work with the epoch theory of child development at Yale gives hope to those who erroneously feel that some earlier stage may have left an irremediable injury. But the main consolation for Christians is to be found less in psychology, education, or developmental theory than in the faith that God can work changes in inadequate lives through his own ways of conversion.

Our Teen-agers

When they reach their teens, a new spirit of rebelliousness seems to come over children to baffle their parents, a fair number of whom live in manses. Dora Chaplin, in *Children and Religion,* has a word for the bewildered parents of this age: "Adolescents are going through a tunnel, and they need to see a light at the opposite end." It is our task to give evidence of that light. Together with other parents, pastors and their wives often near their wits' end, eagerly seek for some understanding of the civil war that is going on inside teen-age son or daughter. The adolescent has reached that age of alternation between dependence and independence that keeps parents wondering which role it is going to be today. He is the unpredictable victim of his own development, seeking to gain the independence of the young adult, yet afraid to grasp it, often at odds with himself and with his family.

At the same time the young people themselves need help in understanding us, their parents and especially their pastor-father. Their interminable telephone conversations and constant companionship in peer groupings are an attempt to both understand themselves and their puzzling relationships with us. Young people have, moreover, an interest in their future families. Not only the parents but also the church would do well to aid young people in understanding ways to prepare for a Christian home. They need guidance about dating, courtship, boy and girl friendships. They need better to understand some of the changes taking place within their developing bodies, in their thinking and impulses. We owe it to our young people to make available a program of preparation for family life, such as that outlined in Chapter 5, for this is the age at which the basis for a strong marriage can be built. Authority and discipline receive an inevitable, yet normal, challenge when the children reach adolescence. At this age they must begin a process of emancipation from parental management, and crises easily arise. As the adolescent shows his independence, often through a type of behavior his minister-father dislikes, there come inevitable misunderstandings and resentments. Yet the process relentlessly continues, with the youth seeking his new place in life by adjusting his ideas to those of his peer group, scoffing at values he once revered, and becoming aware of an interest in the opposite sex. This process is eased considerably if parents assist their young people through the teen years with patience — and a memory of their own youth.

Adolescence is a time of both idealism and cynicism. When the adolescent loses his idealism, he can sometimes temporarily reject the Church, causing a crisis in the manse; and the crisis is complicated by his father's impatience with the youth in this uncomfortable phase. Instead of fighting the rebellious adolescent (something no wise pastoral counselor would do!), he could help his own son or daughter find the way by means of the very counseling insights he uses with parishioners but so often forgets with his family. Some parents seem to panic when suddenly it is realized that the teen-agers will soon be leaving home. In this phase they occasionally hope to correct all their errors of child-training in one short period, which may lead to unprecedented privileges or to a new strictness. David Riesman, in *Individualism Reconsidered,* has poked fun at our capitulation to children in today's America. This is not the century of the common man, he says, but the century of the child. In that direction lies anarchy, and until parents resume wise, considerate authority in family relations, our problems will mount. This does not preclude a permissive atmosphere that allows freedom to grow; but it allows us to be more sure of ourselves and more secure about our relationships in the home. Such security may as well begin in the manses of our land.

The Pastor as a Husband

It is said that Martin Luther got stuck in marriage. After the Reformation had broken loose, he found himself arranging marriages for converted priests, and he often paired them off with the newly emancipated nuns who had come over the wall. After one group of nuns had been smuggled out of a cloister, Luther successfully matched them with husbands — all except one. And she was Katharina von Bora, who remained unmarried (and at

age twenty-six well nigh unmarriageable) for two whole years.
At last the Reformer accepted her for himself with the philo-
sophical remark, " Other women have worse faults."

Whatever his marital bliss (and there are indications that at
times the Luther household was not all felicity), Martin Luther
was strong in his teaching about the Christian family. From
that day to this the home in Western civilization has never been
the same. It was not only the Church, but also the family, that
was reformed in the sixteenth century, and that because these
two were seen as parts of the same whole: " the Church in your
house." The Reformers, who among them had many doctrinal
differences, agreed at least on this one thing: the importance of
the pastor's family life. John Calvin was a cool one who claimed
not to be interested in beauty or loving, but only in a woman
who would " be modest, complaisant, unostentatious, thrifty,
patient, and likely to be careful of my health." But when his beloved Idelette died, he frankly said: " I have been bereaved of
the best companion of my life, who, if our lot had been harsher,
would have been not only the willing sharer of exile and poverty,
but even of death. While she lived, she was the faithful helper
of my ministry. From her I never experienced the slightest hin-
drance " (Doniger, Simon, editor, *Sex and Religion Today,* pp.
77, 78). John Knox, a warmer character, put his appreciation of
his wife as " she whom God hath offered me and commanded
me to love as my own flesh." Luther, not always happy about
his own Katharina, was quite realistic about the marital state,
" the purest life above all celibacy and all singleness, when it
turns out well, though the very devil if it does not." But deep in
his great heart he was a family man.

Today's pastor would be lost without the continual assistance
and inspiration that come from his helpmeet. Before the children come, and long after they have left the home, the pastor's
closest family tie is with his wife. He knows something of the
mystery of one flesh in relationship with her; he will better
understand the grace of God as he sees it at work in their love.
That love runs deep; and clergy marriages are stable marriages.
They must be, for they have several obstacles to overcome. As in

the case of father-children relationships, the pastor here is confronted with a problem that permeates our culture in general, but which affects him in a special way. Modern woman has been engaged in a search to find a new place in society. She has been "emancipated" through her voting franchise and nearly equal employment opportunities. And now in marriage she has a role that grants her equal status with her husband in a fifty-fifty relationship. To the marital life of clergymen this brings some peculiar problems, for their marital partnership is like no other. The clergyman's wife is not only mistress of the manse, she is the first lady of the parish. She shares in her husband's labors, and gives wide leadership to church programs. In some instances, she must assume actual pastoral functions when other women of the parish seek out her counsel and ask her help. This is neither unexpected nor unwanted; but it has brought its problems in a struggle for prestige.

To understand the nature of this struggle, we must turn briefly to examine the status of women in American society today. Woman has shown an uneasiness about so-called emancipation and has sometimes used it to escape the one area where she has an undisputed place, the home. Even our current honor and respect for womanhood is identified by sociologist Robert A. Nisbet as an unconscious overcompensation for the fact of her release from the social role of homemaker, rather than as any feministic attainment (see *The Quest for Community*). She has a reasonable hope now to escape domestic frustration, or to gain some independence that will make it possible to win better terms from man. (Divorces are more frequent today partly because wives no longer are economically bound to abide conditions they once accepted as a life sentence.) In the process she not only sometimes escapes the bondage imposed by man, but has also at times broken out of her own femininity. Where this happens, marital failure can follow, because a married woman's most important role in life is to be feminine, inspiring her husband's masculinity, that is to *know* her mate in the Biblical sense of one flesh.

But the very factors that fit her as wife and mother also militate against these realizations. Her education might increase her competence in family life, but it also makes her discontented. Her emancipation from subservience to men could satisfy her ego if it did not thwart her in marital relationships where her prized aggression may become an obstacle. Her equal status with men in so many fields has lifted her attainments; but sometimes she has gained equality of the sexes by lowering her standards to the level of some of the men about her. Indisputably she has climbed ahead, but in the process sometimes something has happened to her. She is confused about her femininity, and she doesn't like it.

It may be, as Carl Jung has said, that men and women are trading many of their traditional roles as they work out a new basis for understanding in partnership; but it is a slow and arduous process. That this transition period entails suffering is obvious. Yet from it may be evolving a new day in which man and woman not only strive for achievement in a wider choice of roles, but also accept the deeper responsibility those roles entail. There must be some better way to educate our girls and young women of today so that their talents are not lost. Or is it, as one observer suggests, an indication that no one ever takes the trouble to tell a woman how her education applies to her subsequent life? In the case of the pastor's wife, this is serious indeed because hers is a special calling too. The clue is probably neither in how we apply our education nor even in what kind of education it is. The clue has to be found within the woman herself. She needs to find her vocation, whether in the home, the shop, or the office. Homemaking is a calling in itself, and an honorable one. Providing a home, being a wife and mother — these call for skills and devotion of the highest order. For them a careful, though informal, education is essential.

Today's woman is restless. Is that bad? Her restlessness might rather be indicative of her keen sensitivity to the upset world in which she finds herself. The really essential factor is what she does with that restlessness. We can hardly condemn the mother who admittedly grows weary of her children's demands. One mother of long experience puts the truth into clever understatement: "The undiluted companionship of immature minds is not the most satisfying in the world." As a matter of fact, if she does not get away from her children from time to time, they too will sense her restlessness and also reflect it. This, needless to say, is a vicious circle that recomplicates itself until a family is frantic. There must be possibilities for a mother to have time for herself without neglecting her family. There must be opportunities for her to express her freedom and still not run herself ragged with heavy work outside the home. That way lies not freedom, but bondage. Mothers do need to have a change; but a full-time job can hardly be recommended where economic necessity has not forced it. In common with other wives, pastors' wives also know tension at home.

In the case of some women the solution to their understandable restlessness is to be found in outside social and community contacts. Who is to blame them if, after they have spent their primary energy on the home, they occasionally get fed up and tense with family living? But they have secondary energies that could be spent elsewhere; and the contrast would do everyone good. There are community groups of educational nature, like night schools; groups in existence for service, such as the Red Cross; groups that exist for their mere social enjoyment. In any of these a woman will be able to find a place with those of her own age, sex, and interests. The pastor's wife in particular requires friends outside the church membership with whom she can find companionship unrelated to her role as mistress of the manse. Her own education and background have often fitted her for leadership; and it should occasion no surprise that at times she grows weary of her routine.

Here one word of concern might be stated about the minister who marries a professional church worker (director of Christian education, minister, missioner, et cetera). What might seem to be a felicitous union of similar interests can instead become an incompatible rivalry, unless these are two mature, understanding people. The increased tendency of ministers to marry directors of Christian education whom they have met in seminary or church has provoked an inordinate quantity of marital unhappiness. Two people, each trained to do the same kind of work, educated in a school where competition is regrettably but customarily part of the academic system, may not be able to make a happy sharing relationship from matrimony. In those cases where the wife is dissatisfied with her role as a homemaker, or worse, where she rejects her own femininity, the marriage will face odds that are hard to overcome except through patience, prayer, and careful counseling. That very nearly all these marriages eventually level off to a stable relationship is a tribute to the mature Christian love of the two people.

To feel restlessness in these times is but natural. Tensions, strain, and dissatisfaction may result, but these are known to every home. With the restrictions that manse life places upon her, the parson's wife may not be able to make a career as would others. To this she can be reconciled, for she has other, deeper compensations. She has in her life a tremendous and privileged vocation, the vocation to be a mother and a wife in an unusual setting. The new pattern of family living is being forged on the hard anvil of experience. Through considerable *Sturm und Drang,* new directions are being found.

Pastors as a group enjoy eminently satisfactory marriages. They know, with J. Ramsay MacDonald, what it is to repair to a loving, loyal wife and love her in return: " To turn to her in stress and storm was like going into a sheltered haven where waters were at rest, and smiling up into the face of heaven. Weary and worn, buffeted and discouraged, thinking of giving up the thankless strife. . . . I would flee with her to my Buckinghamshire home, and my lady would heal and soothe me with her cheery faith and steady conviction, and send me forth to smite and be smitten." (*J. Ramsay MacDonald, The Man of Tomorrow,* by Iconoclast [Mary Agnes Adamson], p. 73.)

Religion in the Manse

Susanna Wesley was a remarkable woman. The mother of nineteen children (a vital statistic remarkable enough in itself), she herself assumed responsibility for their Christian learning, and began when each child was six years of age to teach him the

Bible in a home course. At an appointed hour every day Susanna would take one of her children aside into her "sanctuary" for a time of spiritual instruction. Her pattern, somewhat archaic and incredible to us, has an *a fortiori* lesson to it: if she could manage such a stint with her eleven surviving children, why could not we do a more conscientious job of training our young in religion? The answer, sadly enough, can be traced to our latter-day busyness and the way that it pre-empts time for duties that keep us from our families. It has happened that a pastor spends so much energy with his work of communicating the gospel to others that he overlooks his own household. One son who went through the unusual procedure of making an appointment with his father at the church, confronted him with a plaintive request: "I've heard you preach on what Christ means to the world; I've heard you quote the saints on what Christ is to them. But I've never heard you say what Christ means to you!" He stayed on until he heard that for which he had come; but he did more. He changed a father's ways. From that day on, religion in that manse took on new life, and was given more time. If a pastor cannot talk to his children about life in God's plan, he is a virtual failure as a parent no matter how successful he may be in other ways.

If it were only information about Bible life and religious facts that we needed for this task, we might work it off with rapidity and distinction. However the process is much more demanding than the imparting of mere facts. *This is education for life,* and only through our interpersonal relations as Christians can this teaching process succeed. Not the memorization of a child's lisped prayer, alone, as Lewis J. Sherrill suggests, but the elemental facts of family living, are the channel through which the will of God can be made known to and put into a life. If we are to guide our children to a mature faith in Christ, we must begin in the relations of our family.

There is a language of relationships that reaches far deeper than the language of words. The nonverbal communication of frowns, smiles, stares, glances, and pats of the hand are known to us all. But we seldom stop to think how much more these impress us than do the mere words that people utter. A child may hear the voice of his irritated father speaking in kindly and well-modulated tones of ministerial patience, and yet sense weariness and anger in his footsteps. It is in the interpersonal relationships of family living that our children get their first taste of community. They begin to understand the nature of life through their relationships in that community which is home. Emil Brunner uncovers the profundity of this insight in *The Divine Imperative* (pp. 512–513) when he points out:

"Education is not primarily the concern of the school, or even of the state, but of the family. It belongs to the divine order in creation that the child should grow up in the bosom and under the protection of the family, not merely as a physical being — for that is a false abstraction — but as a person. Here the child learns (what is more important than anything else it can learn) to know in an exemplary way the fundamental relation of community, the sense of connection through the mutual need of one another, the connection which consists in being 'over against' one another, the recognition of the other as one who is unlike myself, whom I am obliged to recognize just because he is unlike. What the child learns in this intercourse with his father and his mother is far more important than anything that he can learn in school — and this is true even if his parents are not ideal but only tolerably satisfactory. . . . The family is not a school — thanks be — but it is far more than a school: it is community, even if it is this only in a relative and imperfect sense. It is this which is the incomparable element in the bond which unites the individual members of the family to each other. The responsibility of the one for the other, the sense of a mutual bond and a mutual obligation, which this responsibility implies, in spite of all imperfection, is still present, in some way or another, even in an only semi-decent famly, in a way which exists nowhere else."

This conditioning process is so much a part of our daily life that we find it difficult to isolate the elements involved. In the zone of parental influence, a child grows to accept some things naturally and to be utterly oblivious of others. The fisherman's boy knows how to keep his balance in a boat. The considerate father finds consideration growing in his offspring, and the undisciplined parent recapitulates that trait. The manse, as long

experience shows, is singularly capable of conditioning children
for Christian life. It is safe to aver that this has been done less
by precept than through the language of relationships. We
clergymen phrase the bulk of our theological teaching today ab-
stractly — and therefore incomprehensibly for many people. Better by far were it phrased in the language of relationships (as
it is in the Bible) so that those whose relationships have been
happy, as well as those whose relationships have been unfortunate,
might be touched and comprehend.

If this matter of family relations and religious teaching were
a new idea, we might ask for time to set our house in order and
to gear our church education with such insight. But the facts,
less amply documented, have been known for a long time. In
1842, Rev. Horace Bushnell, a very wise man, was writing:

"Or to use language more popular, we conceive the manners,
personal views, prejudices, practical motives, and spirit of the home,
as an atmosphere which passes into all and pervades all, as naturally
as the air they breathe. . . . The odor of the house will always be
in his (the child's) garments and the internal difficulties with which
he has to struggle will spring of the family seeds planted in his nature. . . . Until the child comes to his will we must regard him still
as held within the matrix of parental life. . . . Understand that it is
the family spirit, the organic life of the house — this which marks
by an unconscious unseen power, and perpetually, the silent power
of a domestic godliness — that it is, which forms your children to
God. And if this be wanting, all that you may do beside, will be as
likely to annoy and harden as to bless."

How profoundly we educate our children will never be completely plumbed. Our affection, our handling of problems, our
humor are all parts of a living heritage that our children carry
with them to fashion their own mores and to lift their own
spirit. We once naïvely assumed that children could be made
socially and morally responsible by teaching them concepts of
right and wrong and by making personal demands upon them
for achievement. We now know as Luther Woodward says,
"that children learn to discipline their own impulses and to set
acceptable moral and social goals for themselves in the concrete

rather than in the abstract. They grow up morally and socially by having a pleasant, satisfying experience with someone whom they love and trust, in short, by hero worship, the ' hero ' being most commonly the father or mother." (*The Church and Mental Health,* ed. by Paul B. Maves, p. 141.)

In a task so challenging, it is comforting to know that we are not alone. Looking to God by whose grace we have been called and have been given these family relationships, we make our petition both to fulfill our Christian responsibility to our family and to bring adequate pastoral care to the families of his Church.

> "*O God, our Heavenly Father, who hast set the solitary in families: Look in favor, we beseech Thee, upon the homes of Thy people. Defend them against all evil, and supply their needs according to the riches of Thy grace. Make them sanctuaries of purity and peace, love and joy. Bless all dear to us wheresoever they are, and grant that they and we may follow Thee at every step of our daily life, that, though our paths may lead us far from one another, we may all abide within the safe shelter of Thy love; through Jesus Christ our Lord. Amen.*" (The Book of Common Worship, 1946.)

REFERENCES

In this volume, reference is made to the following books, pamphlets, and articles:

Adams, Theodore F. *Making Your Marriage Succeed*. Harper & Brothers, 1953.

Aldrich, Richard, *Gertrude Lawrence as Mrs. A.* Greystone Press, 1954.

Bailey, Derrick S., *The Mystery of Love and Marriage*. Harper & Brothers, 1952.

Baillie, John, *A Diary of Private Prayer*. Charles Scribner's Sons, 1949.

Beaven, A. W., *The Fine Art of Living Together*. Harper & Brothers, 1947.

Bergler, Edmund, and Kroger, William S., *Kinsey's Myth of Female Sexuality*. Grune & Stratton, Inc., 1954.

Blood, Robert O., *Anticipating Your Marriage*. Free Press, 1956.

Book of Common Prayer, The. Oxford University Press, 1935.

Book of Common Worship, The. The Westminster Press, 1946.

Bossard, James H. S., *Parent and Child*. University of Pennsylvania Press, 1953.

Bossard, James H. S., and Boll, Eleanor S., *Ritual in Family Living*. University of Pennsylvania Press, 1950.

Brink, Frederick W., *This Man and This Woman*. Association Press, 1948.

Brunner, Emil, *The Divine Imperative*. The Westminster Press, 1943.

Buber, Martin, *I and Thou*. T. & T. Clark, 1937. Translated by Ronald Gregor Smith.

Bunyan, John, *The Pilgrim's Progress*. Scott, Foresman and Company, 1922.

Burgess, Ernest W., and Locke, Harvey J., *The Family*. American Book Company, 1945.

Bushnell, Horace, *Christian Nurture*. Charles Scribner's Sons. New Revised, 1916.

Cady, Ernest and Frances, *How to Adopt a Child*. Whiteside, Inc., 1956.

Cather, Willa, "Paul's Case," in *Youth and the Bright Medusa*. Houghton Mifflin Company, 1937.

Chaplin, Dora, *Children and Religion*. Charles Scribner's Sons, 1948.

Chayefsky, Paddy, *Television Plays*. Simon and Schuster, Inc., 1955. Quotation used by permission.

Christie, Agatha, *The Peril at End House*. Dodd, Mead & Company, Inc., 1925.

Cole, William Graham, *Sex in Christianity and Psychoanalysis*. Oxford University Press, New York, 1955. Quotations used by permission.

Danforth, J. N., *The Token of Friendship, or Home, the Center of Affections*. Boston, 1844.

Day, Clarence, *Life with Father*. Alfred A. Knopf, Inc., 1936.

Doherty, Joseph, *Moral Problems of Interracial Marriage*. Catholic University of America, 1949.

Doniger, Simon, ed. of *Sex and Religion Today*. Association Press, 1953.

Duvall, Evelyn M., and Hill, Reuben L., *When You Marry*. Association Press, 1953.

Duvall, Sylvanus M., *Before You Marry*. Association Press, 1949.

Duvall, Sylvanus M., *Men, Women and Morals*. Association Press, 1952. Quotations used by permission.

Eliot, T. S., *The Cocktail Party*. Harcourt, Brace and Company, Inc., 1950. Quotation used by permission.

Eliot, T. S., *The Confidential Clerk*. Harcourt, Brace and Company, Inc., 1954. Quotation used by permission.

Fallaw, Wesner, *Toward Spiritual Security*. The Westminster Press, 1952.

Fishbein, Morris, *Children for the Childless*. Doubleday & Co., Inc., 1954.

Fletcher, Joseph, *Morals and Medicine*. Princeton University Press, 1954.

Fosdick, Harry Emerson, *The Assurance of Immortality*. The Macmillan Company, 1913.

Garrett, Annette, *Interviewing, Its Principles and Methods*. Family Service Association of America, 1942.

Groves, Ernest R., *Christianity and the Family*. The Macmillan Company, 1942.

Groves, Ernest R., *Conserving Marriage and the Family*. The Macmillan Company, 1944.

Groves, Ernest R., and Gladys M., *Sex in Marriage*. Emerson Books, 1943.

Hamilton, H. A., *The Family Church*. Independent Press, London, 1941.

Hedley, George, *The Minister Behind the Scenes*. The Macmillan Company, 1956.

Hill, Reuben L., *Families Under Stress*. Harper & Brothers, 1949.

Hine, James R., and Belting, Natalia M., *Your Wedding Workbook*. McKinley Foundation of Champaign, Illinois, 1952.

Howe, Reuel L., *Man's Need and God's Action*. The Seabury Press, 1953.

Ibsen, Henrik, *Six Modern Plays* (*The Master Builder*). Dell Publishing Company, 1956.

Iconoclast (pseud.), Hamilton, Mary Agnes (Adamson), *J. Ramsay MacDonald, The Man of Tomorrow*. Thomas Seltzer, 1924.

Inge, Dean, *Christian Ethics and Modern Problems*. G. P. Putnam's Sons, 1930.

Johnson, Roswell H., Randolph, Helen R., and Pixley, Erma E., *Looking Toward Marriage*. Allyn & Bacon, 1950.

Johnstone, Margaret Blair, *Create Your Own Tomorrow*. Doubleday & Co., Inc., 1950.

Kane, John J., *Marriage and the Family*. The Dryden Press, Inc., 1952.

Kelly, Gerald, *Medico-Moral Problems,* Part II. The Catholic Hospital Association in the United States and Canada, 1950.

Kelly, Thomas, *A Testament of Devotion*. Harper & Brothers, 1941.

Kierkegaard, Sören, *Works of Love*. Translated by David F. and Lillian Marvin Swenson. Princeton University Press, 1946.

Kinsey, Alfred C., et alii, *Sexual Behavior in the Human Female*. W. B. Saunders Company, 1953.

Kinsey, Alfred C., et alii, *Sexual Behavior in the Human Male*. W. B. Saunders Company, 1948.

Kirkendall, Lester, *Sex Education as Human Relations*. Inor Publishing Company, Inc., 1950.

Klineberg, Otto, ed., *Characteristics of the American Negro*. Harper & Brothers, 1944.

Künkel, Fritz, and Gardner, Ruth, *What Do You Advise?* Ives Washburn, Inc., 1946. Quotations used by permission.

Landis, Judson T., and Mary G., *The Marriage Handbook*. Prentice-Hall, Inc., 1953.

Leacock, Stephen, "The Retroactive Existence of Mr. Juggins" in *Behind the Beyond* collection. John Lane, London, 1913.

Levine, Lena, and Doherty, Beka, *Women Needn't Worry*. Random House, Inc., 1952.

Lewis, C. S., *The Screwtape Letters*. The Macmillan Company, 1944.

Lewis, Sinclair, *Elmer Gantry*. Harcourt, Brace and Company, Inc., 1927.

Mace, David R., *Marriage: The Art of Lasting Love*. Doubleday & Co., Inc., 1952.

Mackenzie, Catherine, *Parent and Child*. William Sloane Associates, Inc., 1949.

Maves, Paul B., ed. of *The Church and Mental Health*. Charles Scribner's Sons, 1953.

Michonneau, Abbé G., *Revolution in a City Parish*. The Newman Press, 1952.

Miller, Arthur, *The Death of a Salesman*. The Viking Press, 1949.

Miller, Randolph Crump, *The Clue to Christian Education*. Charles Scribner's Sons, 1950.

Morley, Christopher, *Thunder on the Left*. J. B. Lippincott Company, 1925. Quotation used by permission.

Morrison, Charles Clayton, *The Social Gospel and the Christian Cultus*. Harper & Brothers, 1933.

Nisbet, Robert A., *The Quest for Community*. Oxford University Press, 1953.

Nygren, Anders, *Agape and Eros*. The Westminster Press, 1953.

Oates, Wayne E., *Anxiety in Christian Experience*. The Westminster Press, 1955.

Oates, Wayne E., *The Christian Pastor*. The Westminster Press, 1951.

Oxenham, John, *Cross Roads*. Longmans, Green & Co., Inc., 1931.

Parkhurst, Helen, *Exploring the Child's World*. Appleton-Century-Crofts, 1951.

Pearse, Innes H., and Crocker, Lucy H., *The Peckham Experiment;*

A Study in the Living Structure of Society. Yale University Press, 1945.

Peterson, James A., *Education for Marriage.* Charles Scribner's Sons, 1956.

Phillips, J. B. (translator) *Letters to Young Churches.* The Macmillan Company, 1948.

Pike, James A., *If You Marry Outside Your Faith.* Harper & Brothers, 1954.

Piper, Otto, *The Christian Interpretation of Sex.* Charles Scribner's Sons, 1952.

Rank, Otto, *Will Therapy; and, Truth and Reality.* Alfred A. Knopf, Inc., 1945. Translated by Jessie Taft.

Roberts, David E., *Psychotherapy and a Christian View of Man.* Charles Scribner's Sons, 1950.

Rondell, Florence, and Michaels, Ruth, *The Adopted Family.* Crown Publishers, 1951.

Rosenstock-Huessy, Eugen, *The Christian Future.* Charles Scribner's Sons, 1946.

Saint-Exupéry, Antoine de, *Wind, Sand and Stars.* Reynal & Hitchcock, 1940. Translated by Lewis Galantière.

Stirling, Nora, *The Room Upstairs.* Human Relations Aids, 1953. Quotation used by permission.

Sullivan, Harry Stack, *The Psychiatric Interview.* W. W. Norton & Company, Inc., 1954.

Temple, William, *Christian Faith and Life.* The Macmillan Company, 1931.

Trueblood, Elton, *Your Other Vocation.* Harper & Brothers, 1952.

Weatherhead, Leslie, *The Mastery of Sex Through Psychology and Religion.* The Macmillan Company, 1932.

Weber, Otto, *Karl Barth's Church Dogmatics.* The Westminster Press, 1953. Translated by Arthur C. Cochrane.

Westcott, Regina H., *The Family Lives Its Religion.* Harper & Brothers, 1954.

Whipple, Dorothy V., M.D., *Our American Babies: The Art of Baby Care.* M. Barrows and Company, Inc., 1944. Quotation used by permission.

Williams, Tennessee, *The Glass Menagerie.* Random House, Inc., 1945.

Wilson, Sloan, *The Man in the Gray Flannel Suit,* Simon and Schuster, Inc., 1955. Quotation used by permission.

Wise, Carroll A., *Pastoral Counseling; Its Theory and Practice*. Harper & Brothers, 1951.

Wood, Leland Foster, *Harmony in Marriage*. Round Table Press, 1939.

Wood, Leland Foster, *How Love Grows in Marriage*. The Macmillan Company, 1950.

Wynn, John Charles, *How Christian Parents Face Family Problems*. The Westminster Press, 1955.

Wynn, John Charles, ed., *Sermons on Marriage and Family Life*. Abingdon Press, 1956.

Pamphlets and Periodicals

Brother Lawrence, His Conversations and Letters on the Practice of the Presence of God. The Forward Movement Commission of the Protestant Episcopal Church in the U.S.A., 1941.

The Christian Century, July 10, 1946, 407 S. Dearborn Street, Chicago 5, Ill.

The Coracle, March, 1956, the journal of the Iona Community, 2121 Clyde Street, Glasgow, C. 1, Scotland.

Crossroads, July-September, 1955, A Study and Program Magazine for Adults. Board of Christian Education of the Presbyterian Church in the U.S.A.

The House Church, by Ernest W. Southcott. British Council of Churches, 10 Eaton Gate, London, S.W.

Kirkridge Contour, June, 1956, monthly tract from "Kirkridge," Bangor, Pa.

Marriage and Family Living (various issues cited), a quarterly journal of the National Council on Family Relations, 1219 University Ave., S.E., Minneapolis 14, Minn.

The Ministry of Counseling, by Carol Murphy. Pendle Hill Pamphlets, 1956.

Pastoral Psychology (various issues cited in text), edited by Simon Doniger, Great Neck, N.Y.

When You Adopt a Child. Children's Bureau Folder 13–1947. Government Printing Office, Washington 25, D.C.

INDEX

A

Acceptance, 15, 17, 29, 58, 71, 77, 141, 154, 167
Ackerknecht, Erwin, 154
Adams, Theodore, 40, 114
Adjustment, 32
Administration of church program, 19 ff., 25, 184 f.
Administrivia, 25, 26, 184
Adolescents, 75, 115 ff., 191 ff.
Adoption, 170 ff.
Adult education, 26 f., 59, 102
Adultery, 104, 142 f., 146
Advent, 47
Aged persons, 16, 22, 76, 153–165
Alcoholism, 23, 153
Aldrich, Richard, 132
Alvarez, Walter C., 164
Ambivalence, 96
Andersen, Hans Christian, 35
Anxiety, 32, 66, 70, 77, 83, 94, 137
Army, 72
Arnold, Thurman, 151
Artificial insemination, 175–180
Atypical families, 24 f.
Augustine, 28, 32

B

Baby, 57–65, 156 f.
Bailey, Derrick, 134

Baptism, 18, 20, 28, 33, 38, 53, 57, 60–65
Barth, Karl, 132, 148, 169
Baxter, Richard, 43
Beaven, A. W., 40
Bereavement, 16, 65–72, 76, 164
Bergler, Edmund, 105
Birth, 57–60
Blood, Robert O., 106
Boll, Eleanor, 39
Booby traps in counseling, 85–97
Bossard, James H. S., 39, 183
Broken homes, 19, 22, 25, 115, 144, 194
Brunner, Emil, 128, 150, 199
Buber, Martin, 130
Burgess, Ernest W., 20, 108
Burkhart, Roy, 93
Bushnell, Horace, 200
Buttrick, George A., 52

C

Cady, Ernest and Frances, 172
Calling, pastoral, 51–55
Calvin, Idelette, 193
Calvin, John, 28, 31, 193
Calvinism, 178
Cather, Willa, 36
Catholic. *See* Roman Catholic
Chaplin, Dora, 69, 191
Chastity, 103–108